COPTS AND MOSLEMS

UNDER BRITISH CONTROL

COPTS AND MOSLEMS

UNDER BRITISH CONTROL

A COLLECTION OF FACTS AND A RÉSUMÉ OF
AUTHORITATIVE OPINIONS ON THE COPTIC QUESTION

BY

KYRIAKOS MIKHAIL

KENNIKAT PRESS
Port Washington, N. Y./London

COPTS AND MOSLEMS

First published in 1911
Reissued in 1971 by Kennikat Press
Library of Congress Catalog Card No: 70-118537
ISBN 0-8046-1160-2

Manufactured by Taylor Publishing Company   Dallas, Texas

NOTE

In June 1910 it was decided to send a representative of the Coptic Press to London to act as correspondent in the Metropolis for the Coptic papers, and, at the same time, to try and interest the general public in the question of the Coptic claims.

Eventually I was appointed to undertake this work, and within a month I arrived in England. From the very first I have met with almost universal encouragement in the mission entrusted to me. I found that influential men of all parties were ready to discuss the question and give me their views concerning it, and the English press were also good enough to open their columns and give publicity to my statement of the case.

In this little book I have now collected in a convenient form a record of the facts relating to the Coptic position, and of the opinions which those best competent to judge have expressed on the subject.

It is necessary to explain that almost the whole of this book was written before the death of Sir

Eldon Gorst, or rather before there was any suspicion that his indisposition was likely to end fatally; and I wish to disclaim absolutely any personal feeling against one who was in every sense a devoted servant of the British nation.

But the facts herein stated are true, and I hope, therefore, that the public will take them simply as facts, to be considered without reference to the persons who may be responsible for them. I feel sure that if these facts are considered fairly and without prejudice, the British public will recognise the grievous wrong which is being done to Christians in Egypt.

KYRIAKOS MIKHAIL.

75 Avenue Chambers, Bloomsbury Square,
London, 1911.

PREFACE

BY

Professor A. H. SAYCE, D.Litt., LL.D., D.D.

Herodotus described Egypt as the land of paradox, and the description still holds good. The Mohammedan Press of Cairo and Alexandria calls itself 'Nationalist,' and the young Mohammedan Effendis send telegrams to the Governments of Europe and ask them to unite in expelling the English infidel from the shores of their country and in leaving 'Egypt to the Egyptians.' English politicians and journalists join in telling us that Egypt is a Mohammedan country and that, consequently, such native rulers as are permitted to exist in it must be of the dominant Mohammedan faith.

As a matter of fact, the Mohammedan Egyptian who thus claims to represent 'Egypt and the Egyptians,' is, generally speaking, not an Egyptian at all. Until very recently his boast was that he was an Arab, of Arab descent, whatever his real origin may have been. What patriotism he possessed was religious rather than political, and his loyalty was engaged, not to Egypt but to Islam. Even to-day a very slight examination of so-called ' Nationalist ' claims is sufficient to prove that ' Nationalism ' means political independence only in so far as it brings with it Mohammedan supremacy.

The genuine Egyptians are the Christian Copts. They alone trace an unadulterated descent from the race to whom the civilisation and culture of the ancient world were so largely due. Thanks to their religion, they have kept their blood pure from admixture with semi-barbarous Arabs and savage Kurds, or other foreign elements whom the licentiousness of Mohammedan family life has introduced into the country. In Upper Egypt, it is true, where the conversion of the fellahin to Mohammedanism is a comparatively recent event, there is still a considerable amount of pure Egyptian blood in the Mohammedan part of the population, but even here large tracts were colonised in the Middle Ages by numerous bodies of Arabs and Beduins, and when religion ceased to be a barrier to intermarriage, these latter necessarily mingled with the fellahin converts. Elsewhere the Mohammedan population did not even pretend to belong to the same race as the conquered Egyptians. The neighbourhood of Cairo was colonised by Arab tribes, and the revolts of the Christian fellahin of the Delta during the first few centuries after the Mohammedan occupation were followed by merciless massacres. If we would discover the real representatives of 'Egypt and the Egyptians' we must go to the remnant which has maintained itself through twelve centuries of persecution, more especially in Upper Egypt.

As Professor Flinders Petrie has remarked, the fact that through all these centuries of persecution the Copts should nevertheless have not only maintained themselves, but have even made themselves indispensable to their Mohammedan masters, is both a testimony to their extraordinary ability and a proof that they are indeed the children of their Egyptian fathers. They have kept alive the old traditions of education and culture through centuries of darkness, along with the Christian conception of family morality and all that this implies. And how much it does imply can be understood only by those who have lived for many years in a Mohammedan country and been brought into close contact with Mohammedan family life.

It is no doubt easy to find faults and shortcomings in Coptic Christianity, and the character of the Christian Egyptian. None of us are free from shortcomings, and it is certainly not for the Englishman, who has never known what religious persecution means, to criticise a people who have so stubbornly maintained their faith and whose faults are in great measure those which are the result of a struggle for self-preservation. Moreover,

the charges so frequently brought against the
Copts by uninformed politicians or passing tourists
generally break down when confronted with facts.
The late Prime Minister—the only pure-blooded
Egyptian who has held office in the country in our
own time—has never been accused of dishonesty
even by his most fanatical enemy; and Tewfik Bey,
the hero of the garrisons of the Red Sea Coast, as
Gordon was of the garrison of Khartoum, was a
Copt. Whatever other faults they may have, the
compatriots of Butros Pasha and Tewfik Bey ought
not to be accused of dishonesty or cowardice.

During the last thirty years I have seen a good
deal of the Coptic people, more especially of the
younger generation, and I have found them to
compare favourably with other nations. They have
inherited the aptitudes and intellectual abilities of
their forefathers; their morality and conception of
the family is that of a Christian people, in other
words, of Western European civilisation; and I
see no reason why they should not again take
the same high place in the civilised world that was
taken by their Pharaonic ancestors. Egypt, as
Sir Gaston Maspero once said to me, is the mother
of most of the ideas that have since ruled the world,
and the children of that mother are still with us,
under the name of Copts.

INTRODUCTION

BY

Dr. A. J. BUTLER, D.Litt.

AUTHOR OF ' ANCIENT COPTIC CHURCHES OF EGYPT,'
' THE ARAB CONQUEST OF EGYPT,' ETC.

This little work presents a clear and dispassionate statement of the Coptic grievances and the Coptic claims. I venture strongly to recommend it to all fair-minded persons who desire to know the truth, and particularly to those who have been misled by British official reports or utterances into the belief that the grievances of the Copts are shadowy and unreal.

So far is this from being the case, so substantial and so serious are the injustices which the Copts suffer from under British rule, and which in a large measure have been created by British rule, that I do not hesitate to say that their position as an oppressed minority is a standing discredit and reproach to our boasted methods of government. The plan has been to show indiscriminate favour to the Muslims—with the not unnatural result of turning many of them into enemies of England and the English occupation, to treat the Copts with stern disfavour, and to turn a deaf ear to all remonstrance.

For, strange as it may sound, the Copts have been refused a hearing. Such a denial of common justice would seem incredible if it were not unquestionable. But it is the simple fact that both the Khedive and the British Agent in Egypt declined to receive a deputation from the Copts, and that when the Copts, who were thus condemned unheard, resolved to appeal to Cæsar, they were informed by Sir Edward Grey that such matters must be settled on the spot. In other words, when a miscarriage of justice was alleged in Egypt and when the local authorities refused not merely redress but even a hearing to the sufferers, the British Government at home rejected all petition for inquiry on the ground that the refusal of a hearing by the Egyptian tribunal is final. It is an extraordinary example of that pernicious bias which seems to warp the whole policy of our Government in dealing with the different races and creeds in Egypt.

It seemed therefore, to myself, and to some other friends of the Copts, that the only resource left to them was to make an appeal through the public press to all those who, in these islands and beyond them, love fair play, and who cannot soothe their conscience with the doctrine that ' minorities must suffer,' when they see nearly a million Christians in Egypt denied equality of treatment and equality of opportunity with their Muslim compatriots. Such, then, is the reason for this book. As far as I am able to judge, its tone is admirably calm and temperate, and the author has been obviously careful to avoid any expressions to which a Muslim reader might take exception. And this principle of avoiding all wild and wounding words is one which I hope will continue to govern all discussions, whether in the public press or out of it, between Christian and Muslim. For, through all the clouds and storms of persecution which have darkened and depressed the fortunes of the Copts, the teaching of history is clear, that Copt and Muslim have no innate antagonism, that each has qualities worthy of the respect of the other, and that the two can live together and work together for the common good of their country in unity and amity.

And on this point let me say one word. It is not my intention here to argue any of the questions debated in this book ; but having known the Copts for upwards of thirty years, I have the highest opinion of their capacity and their character, and I do not believe that their best men are in any way disqualified for holding posts of the highest responsibility. Of course it is an essential condition that anyone holding such a post, whether Copt or Muslim, should be able to reckon confidently on the reasonable support of the Government. But if that can be counted upon, as it ought, I for one should have no fear that a Coptic Mudir or Mamur would fail in tact or in justice, in kindliness or in courage.

But it is sad and humiliating to reflect that the friendly union of Copts and Muslims was practically an achieved result before the British occupation of Egypt, and that it has been destroyed by the policy of the British Government. To exalt the Mohammedan and to tread down the Christian, to license the majority and to curb the minority, is the policy which our Government has not avowed but practised, and presumably has deemed consistent with British traditions of upholding justice, impartiality, and equality before the law, for all the governed. Sir Eldon Gorst, the exponent of this policy, has just passed away, and all criticism of his public life must yield for the moment to sympathy and to admiration of the gallant spirit in which he held his post to the end.

But his departure cannot fail to open a new chapter in the administration of Egypt : and every friend of the Egyptians, whether Mohammedan or Christian, may reasonably hope for a new era, in which the confessed errors of our recent policy may be rectified, and in which Muslims and Copts may be treated with equal regard as members of a single community who have to work together in mutual tolerance and mutual respect for the union and prosperity of their country.

OXFORD, *July* 1911.

CONTENTS

COPTS AND MOSLEMS
UNDER BRITISH CONTROL

I

IN THE HOUSE OF BONDAGE
A SHORT SKETCH OF COPTIC HISTORY

By Mrs. BUTCHER,

AUTHOR OF ' THE STORY OF THE CHURCH IN EGYPT,' ' THINGS
SEEN IN EGYPT, ' EGYPT AS WE KNEW IT,' ETC., ETC.

According to ancient tradition, which there seems to be no reason to dispute, the Gospel was preached in Egypt by St. Peter, who placed St. Mark the Evangelist at Alexandria as the founder of the Church in that country. For several centuries the Church of Alexandria was the foremost Church in Christendom in energy and learning.

One may roughly say that nothing in Egypt is ever what it is called, and its National Church is no exception to this rule. The words ' Copt ' and ' Coptic ' are unknown to the Egyptian Christian until he learns them from the passing European.

They are a corruption of the word ' Egyptian ' and
indicate nationality, not creed. As ' Aigyptos ' was
the Greek form of one of the names of Memphis,
' Ha-ka-ptah,' which was afterwards applied to the
inhabitants of the whole country, so ' Gupti ' and
' Guptan ' were the Arabic corruptions of the root
which remains in our language as ' Egypt ' and
' Egyptian.' These Arabic words the European
tourists have further altered to ' Copt ' and ' Coptic,'
and in this way the Egyptian Church has come to
be known in Europe as the Coptic Church. The
Copt is the indigenous native, the true owner of the
land of Egypt : the Arab is the intruder, supposed
to be a descendant of the Arab invaders. It is
for this reason that all the members of the National
Church refer to themselves as ' the nation,' and
their boast is true, though it is not the whole truth.

At the time of St. Mark's first visit to Egypt,
that country was a province of the Roman Empire, and continued to be so till the death of the
Emperor Theodosius (A.D. 395), when the empire was
divided between his two sons, Arcadius and Hono-
rius. Egypt went with the eastern division of the
empire, henceforth known as the Byzantine Empire.
Up till the reign of Theodosius, the Patriarch or
Pope of Alexandria was the recognised *doyen* of
the Universal Christian Church. There had been
no formal settlement of precedence, but for the first
two centuries the five sees of the first rank had been

Alexandria, Rome, Antioch, Jerusalem, and Cæsarea, and of these Alexandria was generally reckoned the first, while by a canon of Nicea, Jerusalem (Elia) was ranked second. Rome had always shown some jealousy of the precedence of Alexandria, and the more civilised popes of the latter city had generally shown a courteous readiness to yield the point. But the real leadership, and the encyclical letter which yearly fixed the date of Easter, came at first from Alexandria.

When Constantine became a Christian, his new Imperial city at once took rank with the earlier Patriarchates. At the Council of Nicea (A.D. 325) the first blow was given to the prestige of Alexandria by the adoption of the Western date for the celebration of Easter. Ever since that time the ecclesiastical power of Rome increased, while Alexandria and Constantinople were weakened by constant troubles. Rome owed much to the fact that the Arian Emperors did not consider her of so much importance as Alexandria and turned their strength against the Egyptian Pope. At the Council of Sardica in 343 (not acknowledged as œcumenical) Rome had succeeded in getting a canon passed which provided for an appeal to the Pope of Rome as a referee in certain disputed cases, and at the Council of Constantinople, held in the reign of Theodosius, she determined to insist on a formal recognition of her claim, not to supremacy, for that was never allowed, but to priority. Theodosius was anxious not to offend the Western Emperor, but stipulated that his own Imperial city should rank second. A canon was therefore passed at this Council (A.D. 381) which gave Rome the primacy, Constantinople the second place, and degraded Alexandria to the third place in the order of precedence. Timothy, the Pope of Alexandria at that time, indignantly left the Council and withdrew with his bishops to Egypt.

This, however, led to no lasting disagreement between the different branches of the Church, which remained one for nearly a century longer. Though from the Western point of view the Egyptian Church was the first to break away from the Christian comity, from her own she is the unchanged primitive Church as defined by the Council of Nicea, having faithfully resisted the innovations and pretensions of Rome. The separation which took place at the Council of Chalcedon (A.D. 451) was no doubt a political rather than a religious difference. An accusation of heresy was, in that age, the only weapon thought powerful enough to crush the Egyptian Pope. Even this failed. Dioscorus of Alexandria was not crushed : he refused to submit, like the Greeks, to the Roman Pope, and broke off all connection with Europe.

The heresy for which he was ostensibly condemned is known as the Monophysite heresy, or the heresy of ' One Nature ' ; but the name does not describe

accurately the difference, which turns on the use
of ' in ' or ' of.'   The Egyptians, like their opponents,
acknowledged, and acknowledge, that Christ was
God and Man.   They only say that both natures
were united in Him, instead of being co-existent
in Him ; and that therefore it is irreverent to speak
of two natures, as that implies imperfect union,
whereas in Him there was no imperfection, the
two natures were absolutely one God-Man.   The
whole squabble, which had such serious consequences
for the Church, began with the persecution of an
old abbot named Eutyches, whom the Greeks and
Romans insisted on excommunicating for talking
in this way, and whose cause Dioscorus had
espoused.

As Dioscorus refused to submit to the decision
of the Council, the Empress Pulcheria and her
consort Marcian proceeded to disestablish the
National Church of Egypt, and to confiscate all of
the property belonging to it on which they could
lay hands.   This and most of the Churches were
handed over to that small minority of the Egyptians
who consented to accept the decision of the
Council and acknowledge Proterius, the man who
was consecrated Patriarch by the four Egyptian
bishops who had yielded to the Emperor, and been
charged to convey the Imperial mandate to Egypt.
This small minority formed what was afterwards
called the Melkite, or Imperial Church, as opposed to

the National Church.   From this time the National
Church of Egypt has maintained her independent
existence and kept alive the embers of patriotism
in the true Egyptians even in the darkest hours of
her history.   Egypt has been under foreign masters
for more than two thousand years, but occasionally
has made real efforts to regain her lost independence.

One of the most nearly successful took place
in the closing years of the sixth century, when three
Egyptian, or, as they would now be called, Coptic,
brothers, Abaskiron, Menas, and James, threw off
the yoke of Byzantium and established an independent government in northern Egypt for a year
or two.   This was ended by the capture of the
three brothers, who were at once beheaded, and
with their death the hope of freedom came to
an end, though other risings took place shortly
afterwards.   In 620, or 616 according to some
authorities, Egypt was occupied by the Persians
for ten years.   It was subsequently recovered by
the Emperor Heraclius, who sent a man called
Cyrus to assume the government of Egypt both as
Patriarch of the Melkite Church, and apparently, as
viceroy for himself in civil matters ; but the end
of the Byzantine dominion was at hand.   Cyrus
found that one appointment neutralised the other ;
no true Egyptian would acknowledge the authority
of an alien Patriarch nor fight for their Byzantine
masters against the invading Moslems.   They looked

on, with an indifference which has cost them dear ; while Cyrus, unable to hold the country against Amr, made terms for the escape of the Byzantines and left the Egyptians at the mercy of the Moslem host.

Thus, in the December of the year 641, Egypt passed under the Moslem yoke from which she has never been able to free herself, and under which her civilisation, her learning, and her religion have been slowly crushed out. For more than two hundred years the Christian Egyptians or Copts were oppressed by a comparatively small though always increasing number of aliens ; then in the year 830 the Egyptians made one last effort to regain their long lost independence. They obtained a sufficient measure of success to alarm the Kaliph thoroughly. He sent large reinforcements to the Moslem troops, and finally came in person to reconquer the country. The patriotic but undisciplined Egyptians, who for centuries had not been allowed to bear arms, fought desperately but hopelessly. They were driven back point by point to Babylon where they stood a protracted siege. Eventually, however, the place was carried by storm, every male was put to the sword, and all the women and children carried as slaves to Baghdad.

Then the conquerors revenged themselves with pitiless ferocity throughout the length and breadth of Egypt. Many were slain, many were carried away and sold as slaves in other countries, and many of the baser sort saved themselves by apostasy, so that the Christians were left for the first time in a minority in the land. Hitherto the Moslems had only been found in the army and among the residents in the principal towns of Egypt, but from this time forth the country population began to fall away from the faith, while the Arabs settled in many of the villages and began to cultivate the land.

From the ninth century until the nineteenth the history of the Copts is one of constantly recurring persecution and oppression at the hands of their Moslem masters, whether Arab, Circassian, or Turk. Again and again their churches were destroyed, their services prohibited, their books burnt, their elders imprisoned and murdered. As the centuries wore on the Christian Egyptians grew fewer and fewer, till at their lowest ebb it is reckoned that there were not more than seven hundred thousand pure bred and Christian Egyptians left in the land. The Ottoman conquest in the beginning of the sixteenth century ruined them still further, for the artistic industries which they had always been allowed to practise for the benefit of their foreign masters were now almost entirely destroyed.

The Turkish Sultan who reduced Egypt once more to the position of an outlying province belonging to an empire across the sea was Selim I, who entered Cairo in triumph during the month of April in 1517. He forced the reigning Kaliph, who lived in Cairo and still exercised a real though undefined jurisdiction over the Moslem world, to abdicate in his favour, and caused it to be publicly proclaimed that henceforth the Ottoman Sultan was also the legitimate Kaliph, sole lord, both spiritual and temporal, of the Moslem world.

From among the Mameluk Emirs, whose lives had been spared on their submission to the Turkish conquerors, Selim chose twelve who were set over the twelve military districts into which Egypt was divided with the title of Bey. His successor, Suliman II, increased the number of Beys to twenty-four, and issued an edict confiscating the whole of the land of Egypt to himself as the sole landowner. He then farmed out the districts to any man who would bid highest for the privilege of collecting the taxes, reserving to himself the right to revoke the concession whenever he got less money out of them than he expected. Moslems and Christians in Egypt were thus involved in a common tyranny, and the country sank year by year into a deeper degradation. A pasha was appointed to represent the Turkish Sultan in Egypt, but he also was liable to be recalled at any moment, and the one idea of almost every Government official was to make as much money as possible during his brief and uncertain tenure of office. From the conquest of Egypt by Selim to the invasion by Napoleon in 1798, a period of 281 years, the Governor of Egypt was changed by order from Stamboul 119 times, not counting temporary revolts.   In one of these riots the archives of Egypt were burnt.

Generally the Moslems and Christians suffered alike under the Turk in Egypt, but occasionally there was a special persecution of the Copts as Christians, especially in the eighteenth century, when they suffered very much.   At the close of this century Egypt was perhaps in a worse position than she had been at any time since the Roman conquest. Her industries were paralysed, her commerce ruined, her people, especially that fragment of the nation which had still kept their Christian faith, were reduced to a condition of absolute slavery and misery.

In 1798 Napoleon Bonaparte conquered Egypt, posing as a Moslem deliverer.   But the virtues of the French were as injurious to them as their vices, and in a few months they had contrived to set every class, nationality, and creed against them.   The English, who were then at war with the French, followed them into Egypt in February 1801, and drove them out the same year.   But the English were concerned with the French, not the Egyptians, and made no attempt to keep the country for themselves.   The Turks re-occupied the country with the usual holocaust of blood which marks their accession or return to power in any country. Still, things were never quite so bad for the Egyptians again. In the anarchy which followed, Mohammed Ali, a European of Christian ancestry, forced his way to supreme power, and their condition slowly improved. An able if unscrupulous ruler, he employed the best men he could find for his purpose, and the most trustworthy, whether Christian or Mohammedan. This led to the employment of an increasing number of Christians in Government service, since they were found to be better educated, more intelligent and less untrustworthy than the average Moslem of the same social standing. It is true that Mohammed Ali generally chose Copts who had turned Catholic, and therefore were not popular with their own countrymen ; and it is also true that, as in the case of Moallem Ghali, he was apt to murder them when he had got all that he could expect from them in the way of service. Still, he showed toleration to the Christians in general, and since his time no open persecution of the Christians, as such, has been permitted, though under Said Pasha all Copts were treated with the greatest harshness and injustice.

When Egypt was occupied by the British in 1882, the Copts rejoiced in the coming of a Christian nation, and looked forward to a new era of freedom and prosperity. It did not occur to them that a great and civilised nation like the English would be so ignorant as not to know that the true Egyptians, then reduced to little more than seven hundred thousand in a population of seven millions, were Christians and not Moslems. They soon found that their existence was simply ignored by the new rulers. When by degrees it dawned on the British engaged in administering the country that all the best servants the Government had were Copts, and that Copt appeared to be synonymous with Christian, they seem to have thought that injustice was being done to the Moslem majority. An attempt was made to encourage the Moslems to take what was supposed to be ' their proper place in their own country,' and the unfortunate Copts found them-selves treated with studied disfavour and often with actual injustice by those to whom they had looked for help and sympathy. It is true that, since 1884, the Copts have been freed from all *legal* disabilities, but persistent favouritism has always been shown to the Moslems, and this has had a bad effect both on them and on the Copts. The Moslems attribute our attitude to fear of them, and of late years a movement has been got up, principally by descendants of those very Turks who were the worst governors and oppressors that Egypt ever knew, in favour of ' Nationalism,' though the bulk of the nation, Moslem and Christian alike, would repudiate it if they dared, and would suffer greatly if this new intrigue of the Turks succeeded. The school-boys of the Government schools are, perhaps, the only class in Egypt who really believe in or welcome their would-be defenders. Most of the Copts are too far-seeing to be taken in by these Moslem ' patriots,' and remain friendly to England as the only nation which has succeeded in bringing back prosperity to their unhappy race, although she treats them with no sympathy, little intelligence, and not always even with justice. Instances could be given, especially of late years, where appointments won by Copts in open examination have been cancelled for the sole reason that they had been won by a Christian and not by a Mohammedan.

The Copts, who now number nearly a million, are still trying by all peaceful means to regain their natural rights in their own country, but, so far, have met with small success. No doubt it was better for a community so long enslaved that its emancipation should come gradually, and the great numerical preponderance of the Moslems makes it often very difficult to do justice to the minority. But it ought not to be an impossible task for the Christian nation who is still responsible for the government of Egypt.

II

THE NATIVE CHRISTIANS OF EGYPT

By JOHN WARD, Esq., J.P., F.S.A.,

AUTHOR OF 'PYRAMIDS AND PROGRESS,' 'OUR SUDAN,'
'THE SACRED BEETLE,' ETC., ETC.

I AM glad to see that the Copts are at length
coming forward to plead their claim that justice be
done them. A people who have undergone persecution for 1500 years may bear traces of a down-
trodden state of existence of many centuries in
their demeanour of to-day. Still, they earn our
Christian sympathies. Their cause, those who know
them believe, is well worth their efforts, and should
have full support and sympathy from Christians
of every phase of faith. When people who know
them well, such as Professor Sayce and Mrs.
Butcher (who have spent much of their lives in,
or working for, Egypt), vouch for the domestic
virtues and honest, peaceful lives of the Copts, we
can fully trust their confidence in this remnant
of the ancient Christianity of the country.

The Copts suffer from certain disabilities under

the British rule in Egypt which ought to be remedied, or our good name for justice and fair play will suffer. The survival of the Egyptian Christians under the tyranny of Moslem bigotry of over a thousand years is a wonderful fact. There are barely a million of them now—there must have been twenty millions at one time—ere they were crushed by Moslem persecution.

Now that a Christian Power has brought the ancient land back to prosperity, it is the duty of that Power to give even-handed justice to this remnant of the ancient Christianity which once pervaded the whole land from the Mediterranean to Khartoum. The ruins of ancient Christian churches are found all along the Nile, and I have seen, at Soba, on the Blue Nile, the remains of an important church bearing the cross upon its capitals. When Kitchener subdued the Mahdi hordes there were no Christians to be seen, any few left beyond the First Cataract were in hiding from Dervish cruelty between Assuan and Omdurman.

Few of the annual tourists visit Asyut. It is almost a Coptic (i.e. Christian) town. There the influential folk are Copts, and by their industry, honesty, and their intelligence and cleverness, they flourish, and many become rich in houses and lands and are able to educate their sons, sending them recently to English schools and universities. It is an interesting thing to visit the Copts in their

own homes. The Christian virtues are all practised. The man a husband of one wife. The
lady of the house sits beside her husband at
the family meals. The daughters, equally educated
and equally valued with the sons. This sort of
life is a sharp contrast to the Moslem system,
where the poor women are despised or hidden away
as something to be ashamed of. In the society of
Christian families at Asyut I have spent most
happy hours indeed, having been introduced to
them by my friend, Professor Sayce, who had long
known them.

Acting on the advice of English friends, the
Copts have formed a Coptic Society, with a
branch in London, for giving general information
a´ ,out their brethren in Egypt. They have pur-
chased the rights of Mrs. Butcher's admirable
' Story of the Church in Egypt,' and hope to
introduce these volumes to the notice of Christian
visitors to the Nile. They have secured the powerful aid of Professor Sayce, who has been an annual
visitor to Egypt for thirty years. They hope to get
their modest demands, viz. equal consideration with
the Moslems, granted by the British rulers of Egypt
by advocating their claims firmly but modestly,
as 'tis their nature to. At present their children
are compelled, in many districts, to learn the Koran
in the schools which they are taxed to support.
The British education authorities seem anxious to

Moslemise these Christian children, and they should have our sympathy, being their fellow Christians.

I have visited the excellent schools of the American Mission at Asyut. No such system is followed there—but then they want to promote Christianity, while the British education authorities seem to desire to stamp it out. This must be remedied, and no doubt will be. Then there are other (unwritten) laws which prevent Copts of high character and brilliant parts from filling the higher offices such as Mudir (Governor of a Province) or Mamour (Governor of a District)—all these restrictions ought to be removed. Recently a Copt of high position and universally esteemed was elected as Prime Minister of Egypt. The Mohammedan bigots had him assassinated, and some of their newspapers went so far as to extol his murderer into a hero. This conduct should show our educational authorities in Egypt what their system of teaching Moslem tenets to Christian children may lead to.

I wish these interesting fellow Christians every success in their most estimable efforts to obtain fair play for their countrymen.

JOHN WARD.

POSTSCRIPT

Since the above was written important events have occurred. Sir Eldon Gorst, a good, honest gentleman, who tried to please all parties and satisfied none, is dead, worn out with his ungrateful task. It was difficult to succeed Lord Cromer, the regenerator of Egypt.

The Copts are now likely to be treated with the consideration they deserve. Lord Kitchener has become the British Agent, in this capacity practically ruling the whole Nile Valley, from the Mediterranean to the Equator. One of the bravest and most upright of men, utterly free from bigotry and partisanship, there is little doubt but when he has time to study the Coptic question that what these poor folk—the survivors of the earliest converts to Christianity—demand, only fair play, will reach them at last.

They have shown themselves to be loyal subjects and grateful for all the blessings which the Anglo-Egyptian Administration have brought to their native land, and certainly deserve equality with their Moslem fellow-countrymen.

J. W.

III

COPTIC GRIEVANCES AND THE COPTIC CONGRESS

THE question of Coptic grievances is by no means a new one in Egypt. In its present form it dates back to the early days of the British Occupation. Now the Copts do not, and never have, doubted the material and lasting good which has been accomplished since the administration of the country was placed under British control. It is said in some quarters that the fact of Britain being a Christian nation led the Copts to expect favouritism at the hands of the Occupationists. There can be no doubt that this statement, constantly reiterated, has gained considerable credence among a section of the English people, though no more false allegation could have been made. We have never asked for any favour at the hands of the Government. We have asked for justice and equality with other Egyptians, and for a full participation in the fruits which have resulted from the new regime.

One of our chief grievances lies in the fact that we are now denied many of the appointments which had often been in the hands of members of our community in the past. Until 1882 there was no accusation of incapacity to fill administrative and other appointments levelled against us. Gradually, however, it was found that as posts formerly occupied by Copts fell vacant, they were filled with Moslems, and gradually the Coptic people began to view their future with anxiety. This anxiety was not un-called for ; the Copt has already lost much of his former position in Egypt ; he is daily in danger of losing the little that remains.

As soon as it became evident that Moslem preference for the Moslems in the public service had become the recognised policy of the Government, the Copts took steps to put the matter before the authorities. They encountered, however, unex-pected and ever-increasing difficulties. On some occasions the delegates were met with a courteous assurance that the subject should receive the careful attention of the Government ; on other occasions they were curtly informed that they possessed no grievances to discuss.

On January 26, 1911, a telegram was dispatched to London, through Reuter's agency, in which the Coptic claims were ridiculed, and misconstruction placed upon their demands by the inclusion of a paragraph which made it appear that they had no grievances, and that they were working for separa-tion. The following is the telegram referred to :

Sir Eldon Gorst visited the provinces where the Copts are chiefly settled and thoroughly investigated the question of the alleged Coptic grievances, but found that outside Cairo there were no serious complaints. Moslems and Copts, he declares, generally live together quietly if they are left alone, and the worst possible service to the Copts would be to treat them as a separate community. Sir Eldon Gorst found that Coptic educational interests everywhere received due consideration from the Provincial Councils.

This telegram caused great agitation among the Copts, and cables of protest were sent to the leading newspapers. These were duly published in most of the papers and were summarised in the *Times* of February 17, 1911, in the following manner :

We have been much astonished at Reuter's telegram giving the résumé of the opinion of Sir Eldon Gorst after his tour in Upper Egypt. It is very difficult for us to believe that the contents of the telegram correctly indicate the considered opinion of the British Agency. Sir Eldon Gorst spent a few hours in each place at which he touched, and it is not easy to see how he could have conducted an exhaustive inquiry into so complex a question as the treatment meted out to the Copts by the Provincial Councils with regard to their educational interests. Most of the Copts of Upper Egypt (who constitute the majority of the Copts) have complained, and continue to complain, of the injustice suffered by them at the hands of these Councils, an injustice which may be proved by a perusal of the minutes of the

Councils themselves. As an instance of this in-justice : in Assiout Province the Copts pay about 32 per cent. of the taxes, but are compelled to fall back upon private education to satisfy their needs. The Copts have never asked to be considered as a separate community, but only claim equality of opportunity with their compatriots, and that re-ligious belief should not be made a bar to advance-ment in the public services, a matter which leads to friction between the natives of the country. We earnestly ask for the assistance of the English people to obtain our just demands.

Finding it impossible to obtain equality of treatment with their Moslem compatriots in the manner which they were then pursuing, it was at length decided to hold an assembly at Assiout, at which all the grievances under which they laboured might be discussed and placed in a tangible manner before the Government. The holding of an Assem-bly was therefore announced, and, despite determined opposition on the part of the Government, it met at Assiout in March of this year.

The announced aim of the Congress was entirely pacific, it was in no sense to be a Coptic agitation against either the Moslems or the Government of Egypt.

That the Coptic delegates were genuine in their desire to preserve order is proved by the fact that there was no disturbance of any kind during the whole sitting of the Congress, and by the moderate tone adopted by the speakers. This orderly attitude was noticed by the local European papers in Egypt, and also by the correspondents of the leading English Press.

A full report of the proceedings at Assiout, including all the speeches made, was published in pamphlet form and was sent to all influential people in Egypt and to all interested persons in England. I do not, therefore, propose to deal with the discussions of the Congress in detail, but will confine myself to including in this book only the opening address of the Bishop of Assiout, which runs as follows :

DEAR AND BLESSED CHILDREN,—You have organised this Assembly, but the failure of certain people to recognise your wisdom, your prudence, and your sincerity towards your countrymen has caused them to fear the result of your actions. My residence amongst you for fifteen years has enabled me to feel the fullest confidence in your good intentions. I am glad therefore that the Government has once more shown its trust in you. I have come to bless you in the name of the Lord, and to ask you to show wisdom in your discussions and so maintain the best possible relations between yourselves and your fellow-Egyptians, and to do nothing which is not in accord with the wishes of our illustrious Khedive and his Government, whom may God preserve. May our Lord Jesus Christ be with you and guide you in all your actions. Amen.

Assiout was chosen as the best place in which this Congress could be held, because it is the headquarters of the Coptic community.

The Government, however, regarded the idea in anything but a favourable light, and on March 2, the following statement was published concerning it :

The Government does not regard the holding at Assiout of the Coptic Congress with satisfaction, fearing that the meeting there would agitate the mind of the public, and prefers the Congress to be held in Cairo instead of Assiout. The Government has, however, given no orders to prevent the opening of the Coptic Congress at Assiout, as stated by some local papers.

It will be noticed that the Government feared lest the meeting should agitate the mind of the public, and as a remedy it proposed that the Congress should not be held at Assiout where the influential inhabitants are Copts, but that Cairo, where the Copts are in a very small minority, should be chosen instead. How the Government arrived at the conclusion that Cairo was a better and safer centre for the holding of such an Assembly as this, must remain a mystery to all people outside Government circles.

On the day following the publication of the Government notice, which I have quoted, the Ministry of the Interior published an official statement to the effect that :

The Patriarch has just issued a circular addressed to the Coptic bishops and leading clergy, commanding them to advise their congregations to abstain from taking any part in the Congress on the ground that the meetings are likely to create fresh trouble in Egypt.

The *Egyptian Gazette*, the leading English paper of Egypt, comments upon the matter in a leading article on the following day in these words :

Whoever was the enemy of the Copts who pulled the strings to make the venerable ecclesiastic act as he did deserves to be congratulated on a master stroke of policy. The object of inducing the Patriarch to take such a course is quite clear. It was solely done in order that it might have an effect on public opinion in England. The articles of the *Times* correspondent depreciating the claims of the Copts and the inspired telegrams of Reuter's agency have not been as successful as was thought, so a cleverer scheme than any of these was concocted, and the Patriarch was brought upon the stage to see if some really striking effect could not be attained. . . . Of course the idea is that now that the Patriarch has banned the Congress, his attitude will impress the British Government with the idea that the organisers of the Congress are a seditious gang of discredited Copts, who are under the ban of their religious chief and may be looked upon as outlaws. Sir Edward Grey will thus have a sound standpoint from which he can answer any questions in the House of Commons put by Coptic sympathisers by pointing to the action of the Patriarch as completely stultifying all the agitation. . . . If the Copts really contemplate a serious agitation they must concentrate it on London.

That the *Egyptian Gazette* was not wrong in its conception of the construction which was to be placed upon the action of the Patriarch by the Government, is proved by Sir Eldon Gorst's reference to the matter in his report which appeared two months after, when he says that the Congress was unrepresentative and was condemned by the Patriarch. Under these circumstances it may interest my readers to hear exactly what the Patriarch said upon the subject. I append the whole of his Encyclical :

To our well-beloved Sons, the Orthodox Copts of Egypt, whom may God preserve :—We have learnt that our beloved sons are about to hold a great meeting at Assiout of all delegates of the Coptic people in order to take counsel as to affairs of State, and that summonses to attend this Council have been sent out. It is our good pleasure to see our worthy children drawn together for the common weal, and we beg of the Almighty that He will bestow His blessing upon them and give His aid unto them. Howbeit a Council as aforesaid held by a portion of the Coptic people, in a town such as is Assiout, gives us some uneasiness and vexes us, inasmuch as the folk of these parts have no knowledge of Councils among their customs, and thus it may be that an occasion be found for men without foresight to act unwittingly. Therefore our fatherly loving-kindness and our great love for you all lead us to give counsel to our beloved sons to take thought about the things of the Copts in some other way than this, whereby a great assemblage of persons will be drawn to such a town, so that they may have a care lest their doings, which, in sooth, are aimed at the advance in well-being of the Copts, are understood otherwise, and do lead to exaltations of the spirit. Furthermore, we counsel them to have foresight and to weigh well what they do in order that they may attain the ends unto which they have set their minds.

We beg of God to help them, so that they may obtain satisfaction and to give unto them His grace, His blessing and peace.   Signed,

THE PATRIARCH OF THE ORTHODOX COPTS.

It will be seen that His Holiness' objection is absolutely confined to the place where the Congress was to be held, for the rest he invokes the blessing of God upon its promoters.

The action of the Government in attempting to induce the Patriarch to proclaim against the Congress was not the only effort made to keep the question of Coptic grievances from securing the light of publicity. An attempt was made to influence the Copts through the intervention of the Foreign Consular agents. Many of the Copts in Upper Egypt are the Consular representatives of Foreign Powers, and most of them were keenly interested in the proposed Congress. Acting under the request of the Government the Consuls-General in Cairo discussed the matter with these agents, but it came to nothing, as the agents flatly refused to abandon their connection with the Congress, and offered to resign their Consular positions should they be forced to do so.

However, notwithstanding all difficulties, the Congress was at last held as originally intended at Assiout, when our grievances were discussed under the following five heads :

1. As a Christian body of people, the Copts are forced to violate the commandments of their religion by Sunday labour.

As the Government Offices and Government Schools are open on Sundays, it is impossible for Government officials or students of the schools to rest on the Sabbath Day as enjoined by the Christian religion.

The Assembly requested that Government officials be exempted from duty, and students from study on the Sabbath Day.

2. A large number of administrative posts in the Government service are entirely closed to Copts, and it is felt that in general they are not promoted in accordance with their capabilities and merit.

They are conscious that under existing circumstances their religion stands as a bar to effective promotion in the Government service. They ask that capacity should be the only recognised standard for employment and promotion in Government service.

3. Under the existing electoral system in Egypt they are left unrepresented on the Provincial Councils. They ask that a system similar to that at present in operation in Belgium should be introduced to secure the rights of minorities.

4. The Copts have no equal right to take advantage of the educational facilities provided by the new Provincial Councils.

The Egyptian Government has authorised the Provincial Councils to levy a special tax equal to 5 per cent. of the General Land Tax, chiefly for the purposes of education. Of this tax the Copts pay about 16 per cent, and it is felt that in return provision should be made for the education of their children. Under the present system their children cannot attend the Kuttabs or Elementary Schools which are supported by the special tax, because, as declared officially by the Ministry of Education, these Kuttabs, as well as the Normal Schools, are purely Islamic institutions. Practically none of the revenue derived from this tax is devoted to Coptic educational interests, and the children of the poorer Copts are dependent for their education upon private enterprise and generosity. It is claimed that all the Kuttabs should be open to all Egyptian children, and the Normal Schools to all Egyptians, irrespective of their religion, and that religious teaching should be provided for both communities.

5. The Copts claim that Government Grants should be bestowed on deserving institutions without invidious distinction of race or creed.

These subjects were discussed in an orderly manner, and the Congress concluded with a unanimous vote expressing the loyalty of the Assembly to His Highness the Khedive of Egypt, which was at once dispatched by telegram.

A General Committee of 70 representatives of the different Provinces was formed, to meet when necessary for the conduct of business. George Bey Wissa was chosen as President, Khalil Bey Ibrahim and Dr. Akhnoukh Fanous as Vice-Presidents, and Mr. Andraus Bishara as Treasurer.

The following are the names of the members of the Executive Committee elected by the Congress to act on behalf of the Coptic Community :

Bushra Bey Hanna, George Bey Wissa, Dr. Akhnoukh Fanous, Tewfik Bey Dos, Mr. Andraus Bishara, Khalil Bey Ibrahim, Elias Bey Awad, Mikhail Effendi Fanous, Fakhry Bey Abdel Nour, Abdel Messih Bey Moussa, Marcos Effendi Fehmi, Marcos Effendi Hanna.

The Executive Committee subsequently met and elected by ballot, Bushra Bey Hanna, President ; Elias Bey Awad, Vice-President ; Tewfik Bey Dos, Secretary ; and Mr. Andraus Bishra, Treasurer.

IV

THE MOSLEM CONGRESS

It will not be necessary to dwell at any great length upon the Moslem Congress, which was held in Cairo in April. This, according to the statement of the *Standard's* special correspondent, who is universally well informed, was 'held in several quarters to be inspired from a high Government source, with the view of counteracting the effect of the Coptic Congress and justifying Government opposition to its demands.'

Our readers may be surprised at this sudden change of Moslem opinion in regard to Coptic claims. It will be seen in another chapter that formerly the Moslems declared themselves in sympathy with Coptic demands for equality of treatment It is necessary to give some explanation for this sudden change of opinion which was so noticeable at the Moslem Congress, when every Coptic demand was denounced with scorn. It is not difficult to trace this revulsion of feeling.

It has been shown that the Government did everything in its power to prevent the Copts meeting

in assembly at Assiout, short of actually forbidding
it. When, however, the Coptic Congress was an
accomplished fact, a new method was attempted to
counteract its effect.

A counter-demonstration in the shape of a
Moslem Congress was arranged for ; the first step
towards this end being taken by *Al-Ahali*. This
paper is known in Egypt and in England as the organ
of the Premier and Minister of the Interior. This
fact has been declared by papers both in England
and Egypt, and has never met with a contradiction,
either in the columns of the paper itself, or in the
Press Bureau through which the Government sends
all official news and declarations. This paper has
been foremost in the publication of insulting para-
graphs and articles against the Copts since it was
understood that such things could be done with
impunity and would even be pleasing to those high
in office. Before that time it was known as an
organ which dealt with the question of Coptic and
Mohammedan relations in a pacific manner, and its
tone had, on several occasions, been favourably
mentioned by the special correspondent of the
Times in Egypt. Its suddenly altered tone towards
the Copts gave, therefore, the impression that the
Moslem Press was at liberty to indulge in any
vituperations against the Copts which it desired.
The opinion of the Moslem Press that it was in
future to be immune from punishment under the

Press Law, no matter how violent or insulting its articles against the Copts might be, proved to be well founded. No action has since been taken to restrain the Press in its campaign of heaping insults upon the Copts.

The *Times* correspondent, wiring on March 19, 1911, in reference to the Coptic question, says :

The language of the greater part of the Mohometan Press on the Coptic question has become most intemperate ; and it must be admitted with regret that the violence of the extreme Nationalist organs derives distinct encouragement from the tone adopted for some time past by *Al-Ahali*, the Alexandria journal which is generally regarded as the organ of the Minister of the Interior. The contemptuous and menacing manner in which several of the newspapers daily refer to the Copts and to the Coptic claims amply justifies the ironical references to the Press Law and to the terms of the warning issued to the *Watan* last December that have appeared in the European and Coptic newspapers. If the Coptic claims are exaggerated, as is the opinion of many persons who are neither Copts nor Mussulmans, the latter have obviously nothing to gain by indulging in a campaign of indiscriminate abuse, which can only produce a deplorable impression of their political capacity both in Egypt and abroad. Happily, there appears to be some reason to hope that the forthcoming Congress will be animated by a more conciliatory spirit and will approach the consideration of the Coptic claims in a calmer and more judicial frame of mind.

The optimism of the *Times* correspondent regarding the Moslem Congress was hardly realised, as will be seen by the following Reuter's telegram which appeared in the London Press of May 4 :

The Egyptian Congress has closed. This evening the sitting degenerated into a scene of prolonged disorder. There was an exchange of recriminations, a large number of delegates answering proposals by shouting ' Yes ' or ' No,' the result being unintelligible. Many protested against the manner of voting and declared that they had no confidence in the Committee, whereupon the President, Riaz Pasha, threatened to withdraw if the disorder continued. The Congress decided that Mohometanism must be the official religion of Egypt. The Bedouin delegates present declared unitedly that the Copts were fanatics and unworthy of help. Finally, Riaz Pasha declared that he hoped the Congress would bring good results for the welfare of the country and then dismissed the Congress amidst a scene of noisy altercations.

The special correspondent of the *Standard* at Cairo, writing on May 4, the day following the conclusion of the Congress, says :

So uproarious was the scene at the close of the Mohometan Congress yesterday that it was impossible to determine what had been approved or disapproved. The Moslem Press of to-day, however, record the following decisions as having been adopted at the Congress :

The religion of Egypt must be Mohometan.

The demands of the Copts cannot be entertained.

The teaching of Christianity at present carried on in Government schools must be abandoned.

The Kuttabs (elementary schools) must continue entirely Islamic, despite the Coptic contributions.

I conclude this chapter with deep regret that the spirit of good-fellowship which formerly characterised the Moslem attitude towards their fellow-countrymen has been replaced by the intolerance shown in their speeches at the Moslem Congress, and in the columns of the Moslem Press.

It is at all times easy to light a fire, but it is often difficult to put it out. Intense bitterness has been introduced between two sections of the Egyptian people by persons whose duty lies in the way of fostering peace and contentment. It will take some time to regain good feeling, but we hope that the future may bring us a Government which will secure peace for the people of Egypt, and this can come only with justice and equality of treatment.

V

THE BRITISH AGENT'S REPORT

In order that the public may be able to judge the question from both sides, I am reproducing, in full, all Sir Eldon Gorst's remarks concerning the question which appeared in his recent report, published on May 10, 1911 (dated March 25, 1911) :

The Copts.—The complaints of certain members of the Coptic community as to their treatment as compared with their Mohammedan fellow-country-men have found a prominent place in the Egyptian press for some little time, and have lately attracted a wider notice in consequence of the assembling of a Coptic Congress, whose deliberations have been fully reported in England. I may remark incidentally that the organisers of this congress, a small clique of wealthy landowners in Upper Egypt, did not claim to represent more than some 12,000 of the 700,000 Copts of Egypt, and that they are purely self-constituted representatives of their co-religionists an influential section of whom, including the Patriarch, head of the Coptic Church in Egypt, disapprove and deprecate their proceedings.

The revival of these alleged grievances dates from

the assassination of a Coptic Prime Minister in February 1910, but, as a matter of fact, they have been put forward periodically for a considerable number of years, and, though they have always received careful consideration, the view taken has invariably been that they were not justified by the facts of the case. The general attitude which the more Chauvinistic among the Copts have taken up in regard to this matter ever since the beginning of the occupation is very clearly put by Lord Cromer in his work on ' Modern Egypt ' (vol. 2, chap. 36), from which I venture to quote the following passage : ' The principles of strict impartiality on which the Englishman proceeded were foreign to the nature of the Copt. When the British occupation took place, certain hopes began to dawn in his mind. " I," said the Copt to himself, " am a Christian : if I had the power to do so, I would favour Christians at the expense of Moslems. The English are Christians : therefore "—and it was here that the Copt was guilty of a sad *ignoratio elenchi*—" as the English have the power, they will assuredly favour Christians at the expense of Moslems." When the Copt found that this process of reasoning was fallacious, and that the conduct of the Englishman was guided by motives which he had left out of account, and which he could not understand, he was disappointed, and his disappointment deepened his resentment. He thought that the Englishman's justice to the Moslem involved injustice to himself, for he was apt, perhaps unconsciously, to hold that injustice and absence of favouritism to Copts were well-nigh synonymous terms.'

During the many years when the late Boutros

Pasha was a Minister, and still more while he was President of the Council, his influence and authority kept in check the more turbulent spirits of the community, and restrained them from embarking on any agitation which might arouse ill-feeling between them and the Egyptian Moslems. Boutros Pasha, whose long tenure of Ministerial posts in successive administrations and final appointment as premier refute the allegation that capable Copts are debarred from holding high office, was well aware of the true interests of his co-religionists. As a broad-minded and far-seeing statesman he knew that the British occupation was a guarantee of fair treatment to all sections of the population, and that the natural aptitudes of the Copts ensured them a privileged situation of which they had only to avail themselves. He realised that public comparisons and contrasts of their position with that of their Moslem fellow - countrymen might entail changes which could only result to their disadvantage. I am convinced that Boutros Pasha would have been the last person to countenance the present agitation. Unfortunately, since his death, no man of any eminence has appeared among the Copts capable of influencing and restraining the more violent and unreasonable members of the community. As I have already pointed out, the circumstances attending the murder of the Minister who was regarded as their chief not unnaturally caused much resentment among the Copts against their Moslem compatriots, which was returned with interest, and only subsided towards the end of last year.

For some months previously, however, Coptic complaints had tended to centre on one particular

point, that of the religious teaching provided in the
Government Schools for pupils belonging to their
creed.   This question had already occupied the
attention of the Egyptian Government in the time
of my predecessor, and at the beginning of 1907
it was decided to give facilities for the religious
instruction of non-Moslem pupils in the Government
primary schools.   It was arranged that the instructions should be given by a member of the teaching
staff belonging to the creed concerned, if one was to
be found, or otherwise by a visitor, selected by the
religious community, who was, however, to receive
no payment from the Government for his services.
Further, in order to be entitled to this privilege, the
non-Moslem pupils were to number at least fifteen.
If the applications for religious instruction did not
reach this figure, the pupils were allowed to leave
the school during the last lesson of the day, the one
·devoted to the teaching of religion.   The grievance
of the Copts in this regard was that, whereas Mohammedans got their religious teaching gratis, the Copts
had to pay for it except in the comparatively rare
cases where Government teachers were available.
This grievance was not of great importance, as
the amount involved was very small.   There
were only thirty-one classes concerned, with
820 pupils, and the number of outside teachers
was sixteen.   However, as it was clear that
a certain difference of treatment between Copts
and Mohammedans did exist in this particular
respect, it was considered advisable to meet,
as far as possible, the wishes of the former.
Arrangements were accordingly made that in future
all religious teaching, when required, would be

given by masters paid by the State, and steps were taken to ensure that a suitable Coptic teacher should be appointed to all schools where Coptic students were to be found in sufficient number. In order that the teaching may be efficient, a class for teachers in Cairo schools has been instituted, and, as mentioned in the section of this report dealing with the ' Training of Teachers,' a class of twenty-three students of the Khedivial Training College has also been formed. By these classes an adequate body of teachers is being prepared to impart religious instruction to Coptic pupils in all the schools in which there is a demand, without recourse to visiting teachers. Additional posts have been provided for in the budget, so that the lessons will be included in the regular course, and the Copts will not have anything to pay for this instruction.

It must be recognised from the above that the Egyptian authorities have made progressive efforts to deal with the complex problem of religious instruction. It is obviously impossible to provide religious teaching in the Government Primary Schools for every denomination which may be represented there, but, so far as the Copts are concerned, a great deal has been done to meet their wishes, and the Government will always be ready to listen to any claims of a practical nature for larger facilities in this respect than the resources of the educational authorities have hitherto been able to furnish. The way in which the religious question has been dealt with in the Kuttabs and other schools under the control of the Provincial Councils is described in detail later on in the portion of my report treating of the working of the newly instituted Provincial Councils.

To return to the narrative of events which led to the summoning of a Coptic Congress, I should explain that at the beginning of the present year the Coptic agitators adopted a change of tactics, and, while representing themselves to be now in complete harmony with their religious opponents, they organised a Press campaign against the present Egyptian Government and the Occupation as being jointly responsible for the alleged injustice of their position. The opportunity for this was afforded by recent legislation, designed to give to the Egyptians a certain measure of local self-government through the Provincial Councils. The effect of any such development must necessarily be to make the position of a small minority a delicate one, but there were no just grounds for apprehension that its interests would not be safeguarded. The present occasion was, however, deemed a favourable one by the Coptic malcontents to appeal to public feeling in England.

The complaints of the Copts have never been brought personally to my notice by any representative body or leader with whom I could discuss the matter and explain the means by which it was desired to alleviate any disabilities to which they might believe themselves to be exposed. The method preferred was to call a Coptic Congress which would attract greater attention outside Egypt. There were many reasons which rendered such a Congress undesirable. The chief among them was that it must certainly provoke Moslem susceptibilities, lead to a rejoinder on their side, and rekindle the religious animosities which had only so lately died down. The choice of Assiout as the scene of the gathering was also unfortunate. However, the promoters of the Congress disregarded the advice on this subject tendered to them by the Government, which was inspired by a regard for their true interests as well as the wishes of their Patriarch and of the more moderate section of the community. The Government did not feel justified in preventing the Congress, and therefore limited its action to precautions against the disturbance of order. The delegates accordingly met on the 6th of March and the following days at Assiout.

The Congress, numbering 500 members or more, according to official reports, formulated the grievances of the Copts under five heads and discussed them in order, but without throwing real light on the issues involved. Their demands are briefly as follows :

1. Right of the Copts to take advantage of the educational facilities provided by the new Provincial Councils.

2. Recognition of capacity as the sole test for admission to Government appointments.

3. Representation of the Coptic community in the representative institutions of Egypt.

4. Permission for non-Moslems in Government offices and schools to substitute another day for Friday as their day of rest.

5. Conferring of Government grants on all deserving institutions without invidious distinction.

The difficulties connected with the question of religious instruction are not confined to Egypt. I have already alluded to the steps which have been taken to provide proper religious teaching in the primary schools under the Government control. The whole subject, however, and in particular the unpractical outcry raised by a section of the Copts for Christian instruction in the essentially Mohammedan Kuttabs, are so inextricably bound up with the establishment in Egypt of Provincial Councils to whom it is desired to entrust an increasing share in the organisation of education throughout the country, that I have thought it best to treat the two questions together. Reference to the chapter of this report entitled ' Provincial Councils ' must accordingly be made for the further reasons which induce me to believe that Coptic complaints in this regard are devoid of solid foundation. I may therefore, proceed at once to the accusation of inequality in public employment.

A cry of injustice and favouritism in the appointment to Government posts has been raised against the Egyptian Government in the Coptic Press, and found its place among the resolutions of their Congress in a demand for the recognition of capacity as the sole test for admission to the public service. I entirely agree that no other criterion than merit should exist, and that no distinction according to religion be made in the selection of Government employees, or in their promotion. If, however, other considerations may have in the past influenced these appointments, it will be seen from what follows that they have certainly not been due to any preference shown to Moslem candidates. Statistics reveal that the Copts occupy a proportion of posts in the public service far in excess of anything to which their numerical strength would entitle them.

The following table shows the proportional employment of Mohammedans and Copts in the Egyptian Civil Service at the present date :

Department.	Mohammedans.		Copts.	
	Number.	Per cent.	Number.	Per cent.
Interior [1] . . .	2,346	37·70	3,878	62·30
Public Works . .	604	70·64	251	29·36
Justice	1,261	85·15	220	14·85
Education . . .	995	93·86	66	6·14
Finance . . .	1,301	55·76	1,032	44·24
Railways and Telegraphs	2,700	51·92	2,500	48·08
War	307	69·45	135	30·55
Totals . .	9,514	54·69	8,082	45·31

The numbers of Mohammedans and Copts in the various divisions of the Ministry of Finance are as follows :

CENTRAL ADMINISTRATION

	Moslems.	Copts.
Accounts Department .	74	109
Contentieux . .	9	30
Inspector-General .	—	1
Inspectorate . .	12	3
Secretariat . .	28	10
Lands Department .	128	134
Direct Taxes . .	22	50
Central . . .	19	16
Carried forward .	292	353

[1] These figures comprise the clerical staffs in the Moudiriehs engaged on financial work, such as taxation, Government lands, &c., including the 'sarrafs' (tax-gatherers). The latter number 1877, of whom 1836 are Copts.

ADMINISTRATIONS

	Moslems.	Copts.
Brought forward .	292	353
Postal . . .	354	448
Customs . . .	405	120
Coastguards . .	149	49
Ports and Lights .	63	42
Survey . . .	27	19
Printing Press . .	11	1
	——1,009	—— 679
Totals . .	1,301	1,032

In the Ministry of the Interior it will be seen
that the Copts largely outnumber the Moslems, but
the statistics of pay, which include the salaries of
Moudirs, Governors, &c., show that the Moslems
earn a slightly higher aggregate salary—44 per cent.
as compared with 40 per cent.

The above figures indicate that the Copts are
represented in the Egyptian Civil Service, both as
regards numbers and salaries, to an altogether dis-
proportionate extent. Their only possible grievance
lies in the fact that the posts of Moudir, Governor,
Sub-Moudir, and nearly all those of Mamour (heads
of administrative sub-districts of provinces), as
well as the chief commands in the police force, are
occupied by Mohammedans. I think it is fair to
say that in this case, as elsewhere, the tests of
capacity and natural aptitude are applied.

I do not attach much weight to the consideration
that the Moudir represents a Moslem Government,
and has to attend various Moslem religious functions
in that capacity, but I do to the fact that he is
responsible for law and order in his province, and
must deal promptly and energetically with any

emergency that arises.   For this he must be a man
of action, and must command the ready obedience
of his subordinates and of the population.   Experience has shown that the Copt, however capable
and efficient in certain departments, does not usually
possess these qualifications.   He has proved a
failure in the executive branch of the Coastguards,
from which he is now almost totally excluded,
although he still predominates in the administrative
section of that service.   In the Prisons Department
he has also not been a success.   The Copt is an
admirable clerk, financier, and man of business.
Any visitor to Upper Egypt must be struck by the
size and luxury of the houses of the Coptic notables,
by their smart carriages and the opulent scale in
which they live.   It contrasts strongly with the
standard of life of the majority of their Moslem
neighbours.   By their acute commercial instincts,
they are gradually acquiring an increasing proportion of the land and wealth of the country, and
in the villages the small Coptic money-lender does
a lucrative business with the improvident peasants.
In Upper Egypt at the present time the Copt is
prosperous but not popular.   Were he to be placed
in a high executive post, in addition to his lack of
natural aptitude for it, he would find a majority
of the population animated by antagonistic feelings
towards him, and he could not count on ready obedience and co-operation.   The position of a Coptic
Moudir would not be an enviable one, any more than
would that of the authorities who had to support him.
I do not say that an exceptional Copt might not
be found who could overcome such difficulties, but
at the present time I do not know of one.   At the

Coptic Congress one of their speakers expressly
disclaimed any pretensions on the part of his community to the office of Moudir, and stated that such
an appointment would not be in the general interest.
I cannot but believe that this is the only sensible
view which can be taken of this question. As time
goes on, and the cleavage between the two sections
of the inhabitants becomes less acute, it may become
feasible to give satisfaction to the Coptic demand for
more executive authority; but for the moment a
change of the kind would be premature, and destruc-
tive of efficiency.

As regards the Coptic officials actually in the
service of the Egyptian Government, I should like
to take this opportunity of expressing my high
appreciation of the valuable services rendered by
many of them. They have so far held themselves
aloof from the present agitation, and they are well
aware that their good work has received, and will
always command, suitable recognition.

Turning to the three last Coptic demands, I am
of opinion that the desire of the Copts to discover
some method by which the minority may be represented in exact proportion to its numbers in the
various representative bodies is practically incapable of realisation at the present time. Though the
principle of popular election has been introduced
into Egypt, it is hardly possible to devise any
system whereby the scattered Coptic elements could
be specially represented in cases where the choice
of members of their community cannot be secured
by the ordinary electoral methods. The Copts must
in any case be in a minority on the governing
bodies, and they should be ready to trust the British

control to see that no substantial injustice is done to them. It must be obvious again, that the cry for Sunday as the Coptic day of rest in the Government offices and schools is unreasonable ; official business would be entirely disorganised by a cessation of work on two days in the week, and since it is therefore necessary to choose one day, that of the Moslems, who form an immense majority of the population, must obviously be observed. I may mention that it is an understood thing that Christian employees in the central administrations are allowed to absent themselves during certain hours on Sunday mornings to attend religious services, and this rule also holds good in the provincial administrations. Further the Coptic officials are not required to attend on such occasions as their New Year and Easter, while they profit by all the Moslem holidays.

The fifth point presented to the Congress, concerning grants of public money for certain purposes of a semi-religious or charitable nature, does not deserve very serious consideration. In a country preponderatingly Mohammedan, the Treasury naturally bears the expense of such public duties as the annual despatch of the Holy Carpet to Mecca, and there can be no grievance in the fact that Coptic and Moslem taxpayers alike bear their share of this expenditure. I believe that the Copts specially object to a small Government subvention given to the Orwa-el-Woska, a Moslem benevolent society, for publications which are circulated through the villages, and which bear on all kinds of subjects relating to the moral and material welfare of the population. In any case, the amount of such Government grants is not large, and a demand for similar expenditure in the case of a Coptic interest would be taken into consideration if it in any way represented a national object.

I have alluded in a previous paragraph to the fact that the meeting of the Coptic Congress at Assiout would be certain to call forth a reply on the Moslem side. This has already proved to be the case, and a Mohammedan Congress is being organised. Its programme is not yet settled, but the objects of the movement, as at present stated, are to inquire into the general welfare of the inhabitants of Egypt and into the position of the Copts in particular. The Congress, which will be an entirely unofficial gathering, is to be presided over by Riaz Pasha, and his influence will, I trust, be a guarantee that controversial points of religion and politics are as much as possible avoided. But the sequence of these Congresses cannot well fail to have the unfortunate effect of increasing religious differences. The tone of the Moslem press has already become violently embittered, and the Coptic leaders can hardly be congratulated on the first-fruits of their agitation. The idea which underlies it of treating a section of the inhabitants of the country as a separate community, is, in my view, a mistaken policy which must in the end be detrimental to Coptic interests. In spite of the alleged inequality of treatment of which complaint is made, it is certain that, as far as their material interests are concerned, the Coptic minority have never been so prosperous as in recent years. No class has profited more by the era of good government introduced into Egypt by the British Occupation, as is amply testified by the fact that many of the wealthiest men and largest landowners in the country are Copts. Regarding their situation as a whole it compares very favourably with that of the Moslem population, and I have no hesitation in stating that at the present moment the Copts have no real grievances of any importance.

Should, however, a tendency ever manifest itself to deal unfairly with a minority which forms an integral and important section of the Egyptian people—a contingency which under present conditions I do not in the least anticipate—His Majesty's Government may rest assured that those responsible for the existing state of affairs would take prompt measures to check the commission of any possible injustice.

The following are extracts from that portion of the report dealing with the religious question, which Sir Eldon Gorst has dealt with in his chapter on Provincial Councils :—

A serious problem which confronts the Provincial Councils in their educational work is the religious difficulty, accentuated as it is by the imposition of the special tax. The Mohammedans form 92 per cent. of the population, and the Copts little more than 6 per cent., but the Coptic minority is distributed unevenly over the country, forming less than 2 per cent. of the population in 30 of the 40 ' markazes ' (administrative sub-districts) of the Delta, and increasing to over 20 per cent. of the population in 9 of the 37 markazes of Upper Egypt. The proportion of the school taxes paid by Coptic landowners also varies from less than 3 per cent. in some provinces of the Delta to over 30 per cent. in the province of Assiout.   The question is admittedly full of difficulty, and must prove insoluble unless approached in a spirit of tolerance, fairness, and mutual understanding.   Majorities can afford to be just, and minorities cannot expect wholly to escape from the inherent inconveniences of being a minority and should not be unreasonable.   A section of the Copts consider that sufficient regard has not been paid to their interests, and they have claimed that their community in each province should be allotted its own proportion of the special tax to be devoted to schools, under its own control. This claim seems to have been recognised by some, but not by all of the Councils, nor do I consider that in the districts where the Copts are sparsely scattered, and these form the majority, it would prove an advantageous arrangement for them.   I would strongly deprecate, in the interests of the Copts themselves, any system which tends to accentuate the scission between the Coptic and Moslem communities.   The treatment accorded to the Copts up to the present has varied in the different provinces, and it is undoubtedly in accordance with the spirit of the new law that considerable latitude should be left to the local bodies in all educational questions, but there seems no reason to think that the Moslem majority is disposed to approach them in an unfair or intolerant spirit.   Curiously enough it is in Assiout where two Coptic members have been elected to the Council, that the Copts express most dissatisfaction.   Although the operation of the new law is of too recent date to allow of a definite analysis of programmes which are still in embryo, it may be said that practically all the Councils have adopted the following principles as the basis of their policy in this matter : All the Councils' schools will be open to Copts and Moslems alike. As regards religious instruction, the system followed in Government schools has been generally adopted. Where a certain number of Copts ask for religious teaching, and there is a teacher competent to give it, he will undertake the task. If no such teacher exists in the school, priests will be allowed to give instruction at special hours. As regards elementary vernacular education, the Kuttabs also will be open to Moslems and Copts alike, but there will be the usual classes of instruction in the Koran, which the Coptic pupils are free to attend or not as they choose. The Koran is the basis of the Arabic language in this country and its study is almost essential to a literary education. It must be remembered that the Kuttabs were originally purely Mohammedan institutions, where boys were only taught to read and recite the Koran, and that their transformation into places of general elementary instruction is an entirely novel feature. As a general principle there will be *no* religious teaching in the Kuttabs. Where, however, in any village or group of villages, there is a sufficient number of Coptic children to render such a course possible, a special Coptic Kuttab will be created and Christian religious instruction will be given. The Copts claim that their priests should be admitted to the Kuttabs to teach the Coptic pupils, while the Moslem children are learning the Koran. None of the Councils, with one possible exception (in Ghizeh it has been decided that when there are 35 Coptic children or more in a Kuttab, Christian religious teaching may be given, but as the Copts form only 2 per cent. of the population, the concession is likely to prove theoretical rather than practical), have felt able to entertain this claim, which has, I believe, never been raised as regards Government Kuttabs. I fear that the day has not yet arrived in Egypt, though I do not say that it never will, when the sheikh and the priest could safely be allowed to impart rival religious instruction to children of the lowest class simultaneously and in the restricted space of the Kuttab, which in some cases, consists of not more than one or two rooms. Where the Coptic children are not sufficiently numerous to warrant the creation of a special Kuttab, they must be content, for the present, to receive their religious teaching at home.

In most of the provinces of Egypt, the Copts form a small minority of the population, and it is only in Assiout, Girgeh, Minieh, and Keneh that their numerical proportion is considerable. In Assiout the Copts form one-fifth of the population and are represented on the Provincial Council by two members. One has only recently been elected, but the other sat on the Council during 1910, and was, I am assured, in complete agreement with the educational programme adopted. The system outlined in the preceding paragraph has been followed in this province. The three primary schools admit boys of all creeds without distinction. The Council administers 79 Kuttabs, of which 9 are specially reserved for Copts, while all are open to them. A credit of £E.2,000 has been set aside in the budget for subventions to religious educational establishments, and of this sum, which has not yet been apportioned

the Copts will receive a due share.   Applications for
subventions to a Coptic school at Assiout and to an
Orthodox Evangelistic school at Nikhaila are now
under consideration.   In Girgeh the Copts also form
about one-fifth of the population, but they did not
succeed in electing a single member to the Council.
A Copt was, however, co-opted on the Educational
Consultative Committee.   The Council manages 4
primary schools in which 332 Molsems and 78 Copts
are being educated, and a girls' school at Sohag in
which there are 56 Moslems and 14 Copts.   Buildings for schools and Kuttabs open to Coptic children
to the value of £E.7,000 have been presented to the
Council by Moslem benefactors whereas no Copt
has as yet come forward with any gift of this nature.
The principle followed by the Council as far as
possible is that 80 per cent. of the sums spent on
building or managing Kuttabs should be devoted
to Moslem and 20 per cent. to Coptic Kuttabs, an
arrangement corresponding to the proportion of Copts
and Moslems numerically, and of their contribution
to the special tax.   In the Sohag girls' school, not
only will Christian religious teaching be provided,
but the school is closed on Sunday afternoons
instead of Thursday to gratify the wishes of the
Christian minority.   During 1910 the Council contributed £E.142 in subventions to private educational
institutions—£E.70 to Moslems, and £E.72 to Coptic
schools.   In Minieh, where there are two Coptic
councillors and in Keneh, the programmes of the
Councils are not yet sufficiently matured to permit
of analysis, but the local heads of the Coptic community are being consulted as regards the creation
and regulation of Christian Kuttabs.   I see no

reason to suppose that the principles adopted will not be similar to those followed in Girgeh and Assiout, and the same may be said of the other provinces of Egypt. I notice, for instance, that in Galioubieh, where the Copts form a little more than 2 per cent. of the population, the boy and girl primary schools at Benha contain 47 and 35 Coptic children out of totals of 182 and 115 pupils. In this province the sums to be expended on Coptic pupils, both in schools and special Kuttabs, considerably exceed the ratio to which their numbers or contribution to the tax entitle them. . . . It is the essence of the new law that the Councils should be accorded the utmost freedom in certain specified matters, and should be left, as far as possible, to work out their own salvation, gaining experience from their mistakes. The Government will be ever ready to advise and assist, especially from the technical point of view, but desire to interfere as little as possible. First among the questions handed over comes that of education, and with it, religious education. The Government can exercise an influence through the Moudirs, ex-officio presidents of the Councils, and these officials are well aware that the Government desires justice and fair treatment for all sections of the population in this as in every other question. Measures by the Government to exert pressure on the Councils in favour of Coptic claims in certain localities, on account of the numbers or, as would more usually be the case, the wealth and proportional contributions of the local Coptic community, would certainly arouse resentment, as do present attempts at dictation to the Councils by certain rich Coptic landowners in Upper Egypt, and would do more harm than good. The Copts appear to receive in some provinces rather more and in others possibly rather less favourable treatment than that to which they are entitled by any rules of proportion, but the average seems to work out fairly evenly, and I feel convinced that any real or imaginary grievances will gradually be eliminated as enlightenment and the spirit of mutual religious tolerance progress in Egypt.

VI

SOME COMMENTS ON THE REPORT OF THE BRITISH AGENT

In the first place Sir Eldon Gorst announces that the recent Assembly of Copts at Assiout was un-representative. His Excellency attempts to make out that the Coptic agitation is the work of a few interested persons and that the more influential members of the community, including the Patriarch, who is the head of the Coptic Church, were opposed to the holding of the recent Congress at Assiout. As a matter of fact the Congress received the support of every Copt in the country, not excluding the Patriarch himself. According to special cables to the London Press, the Government put pressure on the Patriarch in order to induce him to write against the Congress. What was the result ? He said that he preferred Cairo to Assiout as the place in which the Congress should be held, and that was the sum total of his opposition.

I may add that one of the representatives at the Congress, Mr. Akhnoukh Fanous, was chosen by the whole body of the Coptic Evangelical Church, which forms a considerable portion of the Coptic community, to represent them, and another, Mr. Mikhail Fanous, the head of another family of the same name, represented the Copts of the whole province of Fayoum.

Sir Eldon Gorst quotes from a chapter in Lord Cromer's book ' Modern Egypt ' to prove that the Copts are animated by the idea that, being Christians, they should receive special favours at the hands of the British Government. We absolutely deny that there is, or ever was, any truth in this assertion; but even had it been so, it certainly does not justify the present attitude of the Government in denying to the Copts the rights of equal citizenship with their Moslem fellows.

The late Boutros Pasha Ghali has been introduced into the report as an influence which ' kept in check the more turbulent spirits of the community, and restrained them from embarking on any agitation which might arouse ill-feeling between them and the Egyptian Moslems.' But during the life of the late Premier the Moslems were in entire sympathy with the Coptic demands, as will be proved by the remarks of the Moslem Press on the subject at that time. It is quite true that the brutal assassination of Boutros Pasha was received with bitter resentment by his co-religionists in the country, but the agitation had almost died away when Sir Eldon Gorst's famous telegram on the subject of Coptic grievances, transmitted through Reuter's to London last January, caused it to break out again with redoubled energy. The tone of that telegram pointed out that the worst thing that could happen to the Copts would be the separation of their interests from those of their Moslem brethren. This was surely calculated to make it appear to the Moslems and to the English in England, that the Copts were asking for separation—that they were, in fact, working for some object of which the public knew nothing, and were attempting to rob the Moslems of their rights.

The remarkable capabilities of the late Boutros Pasha, which were always admitted by the Anglo-Egyptian Government, prove how devoid of foundation is the assertion that the Copts are incapable of filling high administrative posts. Boutros Pasha was given a trial. He is the only Copt who has been afforded the opportunity of proving his merit in the Ministry. In his position under Government the late Premier naturally maintained a neutral attitude in regard to Coptic questions of all sorts. He never used his influence either in furthering any demands which the Copts might make, or in opposition to their efforts to obtain their rights. Because of his loyalty to the responsibilities of his official position in this direction he is now used as a weapon against his people, and his silence regarding their claims has been made to appear as though he was antagonistic to them.

The Report suggests that the recent legislation regarding the Provincial Councils was responsible for a change of tactics on the part of the Copts, and that they represent themselves as being in harmony with their religious opponents. It is quite true that the Copts, at the beginning of the year, were working in complete harmony with their Moslem compatriots and with the very best results.

To allege that a campaign was started against the Egyptian Government and the Occupation is to controvert the facts of the case. The intention was, perhaps, to turn public sympathy from the Copts. The Coptic Press unanimously support the Anglo-Egyptian administration of Egypt : the chief accusation levied against us by the Moslem Press is that we give the Occupation this support, and it is incomprehensible how, in the face of this universally known fact, we can be accused of raising a campaign against the Occupation and the Government.

Perhaps the most surprising thing in a surprising report is that wherein Sir Eldon informs us that the complaints of the Copts have never been brought to his notice by any representative body or leader with whom he could discuss them. A sufficient answer may be found to this statement in the fact that a leading Copt, Semaika Bey who is a member of the Legislative Council, a member of the General Assembly, and a member of the Superior Council of Education, was one among many other eminent and representative Copts who interviewed Sir Eldon on the subject on several occasions. Sir Eldon professed his anxiety that the matter might be presented by a representative body, but when the Congress was summoned for the purpose of forming such a body, he met it with opposition and disapproval.

The matters placed before the Assembly for discussion at Assiout were by no means new. The holding of the Congress was made necessary in order to choose a representative body and to formulate the grievances on an official scale, as soon as Sir Eldon's telegram made it evident that he had entirely misconstrued the nature of the Coptic demands. The matters discussed at the Congress were matters which had been under daily discussion in the Coptic Press for years, and they had never been met with bitterness or opposition by the Moslems, neither would they have been met in this spirit on the present occasion had the Moslems been left to themselves.

In regard to the place where the Assembly was held, I should like to ask once again, who are the Copts who were opposed to the selection of Assiout ? I do not know of a single one, with the exception of the Patriarch, and his attitude in regard to this may perhaps be explained by some articles which appeared in the *Egyptian Gazette* dealing with the Coptic Congress from which we quote in another chapter. And I would also call attention to the fact that these articles were dated March 4, whereas the report of the British Agent was published on May 10.

The action of the Government in attempting to stop the Congress was the subject of many adverse articles in the London Press. The only reason why it did not succeed was because the promoters were Consular Agents, and the local Government had no power over them.

The Congress, assumed to number ' 500 members or more ' numbered in reality 1158 persons.

His Excellency, in dealing with the question of religious education, says : ' Curiously enough it is in Assiout, where two Coptic members have been elected to the Council, that the Copts express most dissatisfaction.' This will undoubtedly seem strange to anyone who is not acquainted with Egypt. But Assiout is the headquarters of the Copts in Egypt, and it is there that most of the more influential Copts live, and this being so it is their duty to safeguard the interests of the whole community.

The British Agent is pessimistic in the extreme regarding the working of the Coptic demand, should it be granted, that the Copts should be taught their religion in schools or Kuttabs at the same time that Moslem children are being instructed in the Koran.

In Galioubieh, however, where the Copts are in a
very small minority, this is already being practised,
and with remarkably good results. If, therefore,
it is possible in one province, why should it not be
so in others ?   And also it should not be forgotten
that the principle is practised in Coptic schools
where the Koran is taught if desired. As super-
intendent of a Coptic school in which quite half
the scholars were Mohammedans I have seen the
method tried.   At the end of the day, Copts and
Moslems were separated and the priest and the
sheikh taught their respective scholars under the
same roof. Far from breeding discord among the
boys, it was found to have the opposite effect, each
took an interest in the other's religion and there was
was no suspicion of bad feeling between them
whatever. This is not an isolated experience, I
have practised it on many occasions and always
with equally good results.

In another portion of the report, we find the
following paragraph : ' Buildings for schools and
Kuttabs, open to Coptic children, to the value of
£E.7,000 have been presented to the Council by
benefactors, whereas no Copt has as yet come
forward with any gift of this nature.' This is a
curious, though no doubt unintentional misrepre-
sentation of facts. Anyone who knows Egypt,
knows that the Copts have for many years provided
schools all over the country which have always been

open to Moslem and Christian alike, and that the Koran is taught in these schools by desire. Sir Eldon Gorst himself, during his recent tour in Upper Egypt was present in a Coptic school while the Koran was being preached to Moslem children. It is possible, of course, that he did not know that it was a school provided by the Copts, but it seems strange that instead of making any reference to these schools he points out that the Copts have never actually presented a school to the Government, thus making it appear in the eyes of people who are less informed than himself, that the Copts ask everything and give nothing. Statistics show that there are 2946 Moslem scholars attending Coptic schools. These statistics only include the larger and more important schools, and in addition there are many smaller Coptic schools in villages to which an even greater number than this total are admitted. Also in the European schools, including those of the missionaries, which are largely supported by the Copts, there are 5791 scholars.

In regard to our demand for recognition of capacity as the sole test for admission to Government appointments, the British Agent professes to agree that no other criterion than merit should exist. *In face of this I should like to ask why a recent examination for nine posts in the Sanitary Department was cancelled as soon as it was found that nine Copts were at the head of the list ?*

In a clever paragraph leading up to an imposing array of statistics inserted to show that the Copts are represented in the Government to a number far in excess of their numerical proportion of the population, the Report makes it appear that the Copts have been favoured in the past and Moslems have been overlooked. However, an analysis of the details will prove that of the positions occupied by the Copts, the greater proportion are insignificant and such that the Moslem will not and cannot fill. Also the proportion of Copts in these positions was far greater in the pre-Occupation days than it is at present. But this is not all. In this table of figures *the Copts who hold non-pensionable offices have been included, while the Mohammedans who hold such offices have been carefully left out.* Had the figures been accurate it would have been seen that while Copts hold ten per cent. of the Government posts they only receive six per cent. of Government salaries.

The tables of statistics to which I allude have already appeared in the Moslem papers, with, however, a notable addition. The Egyptian Government handed in these papers for publication together with the figures showing the salaries pertaining to the various Ministries. On examination it was found, in the Ministry of the Interior, for instance, that though the number of Copts employed was more than a thousand in excess of the number of Moslems, the average pay of the Moslem greatly exceeded that of the Copt. This shows that the great majority of Copts are occupying subordinate positions and that there must exist some bar to promotion. This is the question which we have raised, we never suggested that we occupied no positions under Government, but we affirm that the fact of a man being a Copt is a very effective bar to his promotion under the present regime.

I would quote the case of the Sarrafs as an example. All these Sarrafs are Copts, as a monetary guarantee and some kind of education are necessary conditions of their employment. In spite of the importance of their duties and the risks connected with them they are the most miserably paid class of Government employees. They are the tax collectors and financial agents of the Government in the villages, and live at times in constant danger owing to the money in their possession. Their salaries, including travelling expenses and other allowances, never exceed £E.4 per month.

Turning to the demand that the Copts should, when fitted, be eligible to rise to the position of Moudir, the Report says that ' in this case, as in others, the test of capacity and natural aptitude are applied.' I should like to ask on what occasion any Copt has been given a fair chance in this direction since first the idea that no Copt was capable became an article of faith at Kasr Doubbara ?

The Copts are Egyptians as well as the Mohammedans, the only difference is that in spite of persecution they have kept the Christian faith. Lord
Cromer in a paragraph of his book which Sir Eldon
Gorst has not quoted, says: ' For all purposes of
broad generalisation, the only difference between
the Copt and the Moslem is that the former is
an Egyptian who worships in a Christian church,
whilst the latter is an Egyptian who worships in a
Mohammedan mosque.' This being so is it not
perfectly clear that all this talk about the superiority
of the Moslem over the Copt is utterly without
foundation, unless we are willing to concede that
it is the superiority of his religion that makes the
difference ?

In regard to the statement in the Report that
the Copts have proved a failure in the Coastguard
administration, it seems to me that the Egyptian
Government is being provided with an excuse for
a recent action when Coptic and Moslem candidates
applied for positions in this service. Copts were
asked to stand on one side, Moslems on the other.
The Coptic line was then rejected wholesale without
any explanation at all. The reason given for the
dismissal of Copts from the executive of the Coastguard administration is that the Moslems will not
obey them because they are Christians. But even
in the darkest days of Coptic history they occasionally occupied these posts with honour, and, with

the support of the Government, found no difficulty in making the Moslems obey them. The French thought so highly of their capabilities that they selected Coptic officers who attained the rank of colonel, and it was only after the British Occupation that we were told once more we are only fit to be clerks and accountants.

In the Prisons Department I cannot remember any case where a Copt has been tried in a high position. But where there is a will, there is a way, and if it is the intention of the Government to prove Coptic incapacity, I have no doubt it will succeed.

The British Agent makes a statement that he knows of no Copt who is fitted to become a Mudir. This is a rather sweeping assertion to make concerning a community which numbers among its ranks many of the richest and most prosperous men in Egypt, according to His Excellency's own showing.

At the present moment there are Copts occupying the position of President of the Parquet, an administrative position which carries with it control over the District Governors, and if they are capable of filling these posts with credit how can it be said that they are incapable of taking posts of administrative responsibility ?

The British Agent wastes no words in regard to our claim for representation on the Provincial Councils. With no explanation, with no reference to the discussion of the subject at Assiout, he declares

that ' the Copts must in any case be in a minority
on .the governing bodies.'   In another paragraph
he substantiates our claim that the present electoral
system is unfair, when he announces that although
the Copts form about one-fifth of the population of
the province of Ghirgeh, they have not succeeded in
electing a single member to the Council.   I might add
that one-fifth does not at all adequately represent
the Coptic financial interest in this province.

At the Congress of Assiout it was suggested that
the Belgian method of safeguarding the rights of
minorities should be introduced into Egypt.   Under
this system every male member of society of not
less than 25 years of age has a vote.   Every man
who pays a certain amount in taxes has two votes,
as also has the father of a large family.   The holder
of a high certificate, and anyone who has served his
country in a high capacity, has three votes.   Voting
is made compulsory on pain of a fine.   In order
that the interests of all may be safeguarded, every
40,000 voters has one representative.   In places
where the minority numbers less than 40,000 voters,
these may register themselves as belonging politically
to some district where their votes may not be lost.
In this way all ranks and denominations are fairly
represented in proportion to their numbers and the
extent of their interests.   We are entitled to ask,
Why should the application of the Belgian law be
impracticable in Egypt ?

In regard to the question of Sunday rest, the Copts have not claimed that Sunday should be the officially recognised day of rest, as the British Agent appears to imagine, but as already in the Post Office Department, Mixed Tribunals, and the Custom House, no work is done on Sunday, and as by our religion it is a day on which all work is forbidden, while according to the Mohammedan religion Moslems are free to work or not as they choose, it is surely a just claim.

In regard to the schools, I would point out that Thursday is already a recognised half-holiday, in addition to Friday, the Moslem Sabbath, and we ask for this Thursday half-holiday to be abandoned. This has, we believe, already been done in the Sohag girls' school, and if it is possible in one case, why should it not be so in all ?   This would account for half of the Sunday which we claim as a day of rest : the remaining three hours could be made up by a simple increase of little over half an hour a day in the time worked during the remainder of the week.

It now appears that the Turkish Government, after consultation with Sheikh-ul-Islam, has decided to grant Sunday as a day of rest in addition to the Mohammedan Friday.

The reason for this decision is in great measure because the Government finds it impossible to transact business with foreign ambassadors and consuls on Sunday, and also because it recognises that the Christian element in the Empire is justified in asking for rest on Sunday. This action on the part of the Turkish Government will serve to show two things : first, that the claim of the Copts for Sunday rest is a just one and in no sense opposed to Islam, whether from a political or religious point of view ; and, secondly, that there is some justification for those who contend that the Christians of Egypt would be in a better position under an entirely Mohammedan rule.

The Report concludes with a reference to the Moslem Congress, which was at that time in course of preparation. I am in a position to say that it was not entirely the unofficial gathering which the British Agent supposed, and I think I have shown that this is not the only instance in which the framers of the Report were misinformed.

In commenting upon the Report and our replies to it Prof. A. H. Sayce wrote to the *Saturday Review* of June 10 as follows :

The Copts have just published, through their representatives in England, a very able reply to the criticisms passed upon their recent Congress and claims by Sir Eldon Gorst in his Report. It is short, well arranged, clear, and conclusive. The criticisms are taken one by one and shown to be without foundation.

The Congress was neither unrepresentative nor disapproved of by the Coptic Patriarch. For obvious reasons no official took part in it, but 'no single member of the Coptic population' opposed it. And the only criticism passed upon it by the Patriarch was 'to advise that it should meet at Cairo rather than at Assiout.'

As for the contention that the Copts are unsuited for the posts of Mudir, Sub-Mudir, or Manur—that is to say all the higher official posts, with corresponding salaries—the best answer is that they did hold them up to the time of the English Occupation to the satisfaction of Mohammed Ali and his successors. The idea that a Copt is unfitted to govern his Mohammedan fellow-countrymen has been introduced since 1882. If there is any ground for it, this would be due to the results of the English policy of favouring the Mohammedans at the expense of the Christians. When I first knew Egypt, in the pre-Occupation days, the religious antagonism between Copts and Mohammedans did not as yet exist : they were all alike Egyptians. The Copts may well ask whose fault it is that the miasma of Mohammedan fanaticism has been allowed to spread over the country, and that the abominable charges against them and the incitements to crime which appear in the Mohammedan papers are allowed to go unpunished. One of the worst offenders has been a paper which enjoys the patronage of the Prime Minister himself.

The diplomatic fiction that the murder of Boutros Pasha was a purely political crime of course deceives no one who is acquainted with Egypt. Politics in the mind of an Egyptian 'Nationalist' means Islam, and it was not only the low-caste native, but the upper-class native as well, who regarded Wardani as a religious martyr. Boutros Pasha belonged to a people under tribute, and a conscientious Moham-medan is bound to look upon assassination as a light punishment for the tributary Christian who dares to assume semi-independent rule over a Mohammedan population.

Statistics have been invoked to prove that the Copts actually hold more than their proportionate share of the official posts in Egypt. If they did there would be some justification for it, as they possess a large part of the property and most of the brains of the country. But as a matter of fact they are excluded, not only from the higher administra-tive posts, but also from a considerable portion of the pensionable ones, and the statistics have been so manipulated as to produce a wholly wrong impression of the actual facts. In the Report the Copts who hold non-pensionable offices have been included, while the Mohammedans who hold them have been carefully excluded. If the statistics had been accurately given, it would have been found that while the Copts are in receipt of 10 per cent. of the Government posts they get only 6 per cent. of the pay.

The most serious complaint, however, which the Copts have to bring against the existing order of things is that which relates to education. Pro-vincial Councils have lately been established, and they have been authorised to levy a supertax equal to 5 per cent. of the General Land Tax, chiefly for the purposes of education. Of this the Copts pay about 16 per cent., and they feel that in return some provision should be made for the educa-tion of their children. The British Agent tells them

to send the children to the Government schools;
but these schools are purely Islamic institutions, in
which the Quoran is made the basis of instruction.
No Christian who believes his own religion and has
a first-hand acquaintance with Mohammedanism and
it effects upon the young, could let his children go to
them. Of course it is said that Arabic cannot be
properly taught without using the Quoran as a
text-book; to this it is sufficient to reply that it
is taught efficiently without doing anything of the
kind in the Jesuit and American Schools. By all
means let the Quoran be studied—scientifically,
that is to say—in the secondary schools, but to
make it the foundation of teaching in the primary
schools is to introduce a more effective method of
forcing the Christian remnant in Egypt to forsake
their religion than all the Mohammedan persecu-
tions of the past. And to tax the Coptic parent in
order that his children may be turned into Mohammedans is going a little too far. The invention of
the scheme says much for the ingenuity of that
great Mohammedanising power, the British control.

Some further facts on this subject are given in a
pamphlet published by the Committee of the Coptic
Congress. In reference to the statement that the
Assembly did not represent more than 12,000
persons the Committee says the fact is, that the
1158 delegates had between them 10,500 proxies.
This is probably the number alluded to in the
Report when it states that the Assembly did not
claim to represent more than 12,000 persons. These

proxies were not representative of one person only, as was evidently supposed, but some represented a hundred, and some as many as a thousand signatures.

Another point of great importance alleged against the Copts is that, instead of approaching the Government or the British Agent in a constitutional manner, they preferred to hold a Congress for the sake of publicity.   On June 25, 1908, Dr. Akhnoukh Fanous, LL.D., President of the Reform League, and head of the Evangelical Coptic Church, wrote to the British Agent asking for permission to lay before him a statement of the Coptic grievances, and he received the following reply from the Secretary to the British Agency, dated June 29, 1908 :

I am directed by Sir Eldon Gorst to inform you that he has received your letter dated the 25th inst. and has noted its contents.

No further notice was taken of the appeal. On June 20, 1910, a leading Coptic Society, known as the Tewfik Society, asked for an interview on the Education Question, and received an answer, dated June 23, 1910, as follows :

I am directed by Sir Eldon Gorst to acknowledge your letter of the 20th inst., and to remind you that the questions raised are already under consideration by the Egyptian Government, which will, he does not doubt, arrive at a satisfactory solution of the existing difficulties. He will, however, be happy to listen to any observations you may have to make upon whatever arrangement is ultimately determined.

As no arrangement was ever 'ultimately determined,' the Society was, naturally, never called upon for its 'observations.' After the conclusion of the Congress the Executive Committee drew up the form in which the requests agreed upon should be submitted. A letter was then addressed to the British Agent requesting him to give the Committee an opportunity of presenting their requests. No reply was received to this, but the British Agent's Secretary verbally informed a member of the Committee that the British Agent was unwilling to receive a deputation. Before writing to Sir Eldon Gorst the Executive Committee had communicated with the Master of Ceremonies of the Khedive and requested him to arrange an audience with His Highness. In reply to this the Master of Ceremonies summoned the President to the palace and informed him that the Khedive was unable to receive a deputation, as the Assembly had not been authorised by the Government and also because some of its leaders were Consular Agents of Foreign Powers.

It was stated in the Report that one of the speakers at the Coptic Congress admitted in his speech that the appointment of Copts to administrative posts was not for the general interest. What the speaker actually said was that he looked upon the appointment of Copts to administrative posts as a loss to themselves, and he wished that all Copts were out of Government offices and working independently, as this would be more to their advantage financially.

It has already been pointed out that the Moslems had no objection to the appointment of Copts to administrative positions before the British authorities spread the idea that they were not fit for them ; but the Committee in their reply point out the interesting fact that the reasons given at the Moslem Congress for the objections are precisely those that appear in the Report of the Agent. This Report was written a month before the Congress was held, but was only made public ten days after the Congress closed. The arguments on the subject of education are also identical with those found in the Report, which the public was not supposed to see until some time afterwards.

The table of statistics, which occupies such an important place in the Report, appeared in much greater detail in the Mohammedan papers one month before the publication of that Report. It is quite obvious that these statistics could only have been obtained from high official sources, and the manner in which they were set forth was calculated to cause ill-feeling, and so foster the promotion of the Mohammedan Congress directed against the Coptic community.

A very remarkable thing is that, whereas in the Government schools it is possible to teach both religions, it is supposed to be impossible in the village schools or Kuttabs, where one would expect the children, being younger, to be more under control.

According to the British Agent the Egyptians are not yet ready to receive religious teaching without trouble, but these same people were considered by a Moslem Khedive to be quite ready for this in 1863. In that year the Khedive, Ismail Pasha, set aside 28,000 acres of land to endow a system of elementary teaching, and one of the articles of his decree is as follows :

Article 3.—These Kuttabs must be open to all classes and all members of different religions equally. As it is absolutely necessary to teach Mohammedan and Coptic children the principles of their religions, there must be in every Kuttab a room in which the Copts may be taught their religion by a priest appointed by the Patriarch, and another where a sheikh can teach the principles of the Mohammedan religion. For the rest of the teaching both communities will work together.

Thus it appears that, so far from asking for new favours, the Copts are, in this case at all events, merely seeking to get back the advantages they enjoyed when the land was entirely under Moslem control.

In answer to the suggestion that the Copts are free to attend any of the Moslem Kuttabs it is sufficient to point out that these establishments are entirely Mohammedan institutions, where children are taught to read and recite the Koran, as is mentioned in the Report, and four hours out of the six are daily devoted to purely Mohammedan subjects. A Coptic child attending such a school would either have to learn Mohammedanism instead of the Christian religion, or else waste four hours out of the six school hours daily.

Finally, as an instance of the favouritism and bias which have been for some time sufficiently evident on the part of the authorities, the Committee allege that on May 1 His Highness the Khedive left Cairo for Alexandria, and when passing Tantah he had a conversation with the Moudir of the province of Gharbieh. He stated that his departure from Cairo had been fixed for April 29, but he afterwards noticed that this was the date for opening the Mohammedan Congress. As he feared his leaving then might be taken as an expression of disapproval of the Congress, he had postponed his departure until May 1. He expressed himself as highly pleased with the work of the Congress.

It will be remembered that His Highness refused to have anything to do with or say to the proposed deputation from the Coptic Congress.

VII

THE QUESTION IN PARLIAMENT

In order that my readers may be at one with their subject I am appending the details of all questions concerning the subject which have been asked in Parliament up to the present day :

On February 24, 1911, Sir William Bull asked the Secretary of State for Foreign Affairs ' whether he has recently received petitions from various sections of the Coptic community in Egypt, drawing attention to the religious disabilities from which they now suffer, particularly in regard to elementary education in the Kuttabs ; and whether he has received any information to show that these grievances are receiving proper attention from the authorities, independently of the Provincial Councils, with a view to their redress.'

Sir E. Grey : ' I have received telegrams on this subject from four Coptic communities in Egypt, and have referred them to His Majesty's Agent, and Consul-General at Cairo for report.'

On February 28, 1911, Mr. Ormsby-Gore asked ' whether the Government has recently received any memorial from the Coptic population in Egypt dealing with various grievances chiefly owing to religious disabilities in educational matters ; whether the Government of Egypt are about to deal with these grievances ; and whether he will shortly lay papers on the subject.'

Sir Edward Grey : ' I would refer the hon. member to the reply I made to the question of the hon. member for Hammersmith on the 24th instant. I must await Sir Eldon Gorst's report before making any statement on the subject.'

On March 9, 1911, Mr. Ormsby-Gore asked the Secretary of State for Foreign Affairs ' whether his attention had been called to a meeting of the General Coptic Assembly at Assiout on Monday, March 6, and to the allegation that difficulties arose between the Coptic authorities and the Egyptian Government as to the place and character of the meeting ; whether he has received from Egypt any reports as to the objects and conduct of the meetings ; and whether he has received any communications criticising the action of the Egyptian Government in connection with the meetings of the Coptic Committee or Coptic General Assembly.'

Sir Edward Grey : ' The reply to all the hon. member's questions is in the negative.'

On March 28, 1911, Mr. Ormsby-Gore asked the Secretary of State for Foreign Affairs ' what newspapers have been warned by the Egyptian Government in the last six months under the Press Acts, and for what reasons ; and which newspapers so warned have subsequently been suppressed.'

Sir Edward Grey : ' The *Lewa* and *Watan* have both been warned, but I cannot give a complete reply without time for further inquiry.'

On May 16, 1911, Mr. Ormsby-Gore asked the Secretary of State 'whether the complaints, if any, of the Coptic community in Egypt have ever been brought personally to his notice, or to the notice of His Majesty's Agent-General in Egypt, by any accredited representative of the Coptic community or Coptic Congress; and whether any such Coptic representative has ever made any request to place the views of Copts personally before him or His Majesty's Agent-General.'

Sir Edward Grey: 'As far as His Majesty's Consul-General in Egypt is concerned, the answer about the complaints of the Copts is contained in Sir Eldon Gorst's report, and I entirely approve of what he says. I have received a request for a personal interview from Mr. Fanous, who stated that he had been authorised by the Coptic Congress to represent their views, but I consider it better that the question should be dealt with in Egypt.'

On July 27, when the House was in Committee on Supply, a debate took place. Col. Williams spoke as follows: 'I wish to address one word to the Foreign Secretary in reference to a matter which arose when Lord Cromer was in Egypt. It is concerned with the administration of Mohammedan countries, where, although we are administering for the Mohammedan people, we must remember that not only is there a considerable number of English people in Egypt, but that there is also that ancient Christian Church of the Copts which has suffered and is suffering from what its members feel to be a grievance. In view of the appointment of Lord Kitchener I trust that this will no longer be so. Lord Cromer started with the idea that Friday was the Mohammedan Sunday, and that

Egypt being a Mohammedan country, Friday was
to be observed by Christian people as the weekly
rest day, and not the Christian Sunday.   Of course
anybody who knows anything about Mohammedans
knows that Friday is the day on which Mohammedans
go to the Mosque.   But he also knows that it is not
a day on which the Mohammedan leaves any bit
of business he has in hand or makes any alteration
in his secular life such as the Sunday imposes upon
Christian people.   The result has been that Christian
officers and Englishmen—who are Christian of
course—who are employed in Egypt are obliged to
work the whole of the Sunday.   The same is the
case with the Copts, who wish to observe the Sunday
for themselves, but are often deprived of the opportunity of attending their own places of worship
because Sunday is not a *dies non* in the Egyptian
offices, as it would be in England among our own
people ; and they are positively unable to observe
the holiday as a day of rest and religious obligation,
while they are obliged to observe Friday, whether
they like it or not.   I hope that the Foreign Secretary will take this matter into consideration, and
will discuss with Lord Kitchener if it is possible to
make some change which would meet the position
of a very large section of the people who belong to
that very ancient Christian Church, the Copts, and
also of the many other Christian people who live
in Egypt.   There is no reason that we should forget
the obligations of our own religion.'

On August 16, 1911, in the House of Commons,
Mr. Keir Hardie asked the Secretary of State for
Foreign Affairs ' whether any discrimination is shown
as between Christians and Mohammedans in making
appointments to the Civil Service in Egypt, or

whether instructions have been issued to the representative of His Majesty in Egypt to discriminate
in the making of such appointments between the
members of the two communities named.'

The Under-Secretary of State for Foreign Affairs
(Mr. McKinnon Wood): 'I would refer the hon.
Member to the late Sir Eldon Gorst's last Annual
Report on Egypt, Part 5, where he fully deals with
the question of the proportional employment of
Mohammedans and Copts in the Egyptian Civil
Service. No instructions in the sense suggested in
the last part of the question have been or will be
sent to His Majesty's representative in Egypt.'

It is not, of course, surprising that all replies
concerning the Egyptian Government's treatment
of Copts have been given in favour of the British
Agent. It would be impossible for him to retain
his position without the support of the Home
Government. It is easy for Sir Edward Grey
to refer us to Egypt, but we must not lose
sight of the fact that it was only after we had
exhausted every possible means of obtaining satisfaction in Egypt without result that we turned
our attention to England. We recently asked
permission to present our grievances to the British
Agency, but this was refused. This request was, it is
true, made after the departure of the British Agent
for Europe on leave, but the matter had been brought
to his personal notice on more than one occasion
by certain leading members of the Coptic community.

VIII

MOSLEM OPINION

One of our greatest grievances lies in the fact that the policy lately pursued by the Government has alienated Moslem from Coptic sympathies in Egypt. For many years the good understanding between us had been such that the Moslems were quite ready to recognise the justice of our demands, as will be proved by the following few extracts from the Moslem Press prior to the recent declaration against the Copts on the part of the authorities.

Al-Moayad, the organ of the Constitutional Party, May 1908, says :

We cannot understand why the Copts do not take their share in the administrative positions, as natives have all national rights equally. . . . It might be imagined that the Mudir must be a Moslem, because he presides at the religious ceremonies and prays on Friday with the Khedive on official visits ; but this is not enough to prevent the Copt from being promoted to an office of which he is capable and fit to fill. There is a sub-Mudir, who could take all religious ceremonies. We say this and ask the Government, which is solely responsible for it, to remove all differences.

Al-Lewa, the organ of the Nationalist Party, May 1908, says :

We, the Moslems, heartily wish that the Government appointments should be given to those deserving them, without making any difference between one religion and another.

Al-Gerida, one of the principal Moslem papers, and the organ of the Party of the People, May 1908, says :

Our opinion concerning equality between Copts and Moslems is well known through our many statements on the subject, and we say that every Egyptian has the right of general equality without difference.

And the following is an extract from an article which appeared in the same paper, in reply to an article by Dr. A. J. Butler which was published in the October number of the *Nineteenth Century*, 1910 :

There is no doubt but that the British Occupation is the creator of bad feeling between Copts and Moslems. No one, not even Dr. Butler himself, could question the fact that Lord Cromer favoured one section of the Egyptian people more than another for political reasons, and this policy was evident to all.

Misr-el-Fatat, the most fanatical Mohammedan paper, in the issue of January 29, 1911, put the following question to the Copts concerning their grievance—that Moslems were shown preference in regard to Government appointments :

Are the Moslems responsible for the manner in which the Copts are withheld from the holding of appointments and denied the right of promotion according to their capabilities, or is not rather the Occupation responsible for this treatment : the Occupation, whom the Copts laud and worship, pretending that the evacuation by the British would mean disaster to their interests, thus proving that they are enemies of the Constitution and haters of liberty ? Do they still think, after the failure of their representative in England and the refusal of their demands, after the *Times* newspaper has declared that the Copts are incapable of holding administrative posts, do they still think, after all this, that it is the Moslems who deny their capabilities, or is it the British who do so ?

Soliman Obaid, a prominent Moslem, who formerly held the position of District Governor in Egypt, in the course of a letter to *Al-Watan* newspaper, in its issue of November 23, 1910, writes as follows :

I have spent years in the company of my brethren the Copts, and am still in touch with them. They are loyal to their religion, and are deeply appreciative of any favour shown to them. They have every sympathy with their friends, entering heartily into their joys or sorrows. When a Copt quarrels with a Moslem he bears him no ill-will, and would never take advantage of an opportunity to do him harm. If his forgiveness is asked, he gives it fully, in accordance with the law laid down by the Christ. I have seen on more than one occasion the Coptic chief clerks in the provinces use their influence to secure promotion for Moslems in the Government service, despite the fact that there were men of their own nationality capable of filling the positions as they fell vacant. I once asked one of the chief clerks why he promoted a Moslem to a position for which a Copt, who was senior in the service and was better qualified to fill, had applied. He replied that the qualifications of the two men were almost equal, but that the family of the Moslem candidate was numerous, though the Copt had more years of service. I may add that I never found the Copts working against their Moslem inferiors in any way, but, on the contrary, I have always found them to be sympathetic and ready and willing to condone offences. They always try to avoid the fanaticism which some of the Moslem employees when they fall into disgrace use as a weapon against their Coptic employers. The Copts are never found to be avaricious, but, on the contrary, they devote much money for the benefit of the poor, Copts and Moslems alike, and they also give liberally to schools, hospitals, &c., which are open to both Copts and Moslems. They have trained themselves to perfection. I have noticed recently that some of the Moslem papers have called attention to the number of Copts employed

in the Ministries of Finance, Post Office, and Rail-
ways. And also they attack the Copts as asking
favours of the Government, and accuse them of
being traitors to the country because they will not
join in the agitation for a Constitution. It is a
well-known fact that our brethren the Copts have
been employed for the clerical and accountant's
work of the Government for ages past. We, the
Moslems, have, until recent years, been quite incapable of doing clerical work, and we still dislike
accountancy; some of us call it 'hard labour,' others
'dirty work,' and for these reasons the Copts have a
great share of this work. It is for this reason and
for no other that the Copts are now so numerous
in these departments. The heads of the Government departments are Moslems, and the Copts did
not obtain their positions by force. Although their
numbers in Government appointments are very
great, nearly all their positions are very small, with
very low pay. The work is really hard : this can
be proved by the fact that at the present moment
there are many Moslems who are learned in figures
yet who will not take the positions now occupied
by Copts because they consider the work too hard
for them. I consider the Copts do their best not to
hurt our feelings, and they always take part in our
works of benevolence. Concerning the tone of the
Moslem Press, I think that their violent articles are
meant only to deceive the simple and to gain the
assistance of the foolish wealthy. They utter a cry
with their lips which does not come from their
hearts. They shout for the Constitution, but if it
came Egypt would relapse into a state of anarchy.
We now have complete liberty, which could not be

ours under a constitutional Government. Before the Occupation we had no Government similar to the present day, and the good which it has brought to Egypt is evident everywhere in the country. I cannot understand why one sees constantly one article after another in the local press attacking my brethren the Copts because they ask for equality of treatment in the matter of appointments. Are these claims not just, considering that the Copts are our native brethren, having equal rights with our own ? Why should they not make these just claims ? They have energy and intelligence and are capable of holding the highest positions. Are they barred from promotion because it is said that the majority are Moslems ? I believe that in making these statements we expose ourselves in the papers of other nations as being unwilling that their rights of equality should be recognised. This is against the will of God and the public peace.

Although it will be seen that the above letter was published some considerable time before the Report of 1911 was written, I think it will be found to constitute an excellent reply to some of the remarks on the Coptic question contained in that Report.

Anis Bey, one of the most influential Moslems in Egypt, stated in the Cairo newspaper *Ahram*, in July 1910, that Moslems have the greatest respect for Coptic officials, and never doubt or question their ability, integrity, or honour : and when Moslems have disputes among themselves they employ

Coptic barristers. Many powerful Moslems employ Copts in their private offices in the most confidential positions and trust them implicitly.

Thus it is very clear that, left to themselves, the Egyptians are capable of settling their differences or rather forgetting that there are any. And, indeed, as the only difference is the essentially private one of religious belief, there seems no reason why any bad feeling should exist. But the partial attitude of the Egyptian Government, the continual preaching, both by word and deed, of the pernicious doctrine that the Copt was only useful as a clerk or accountant, and of no manner of service as a person of authority, could not fail to have its effect. Gradually the Moslem Press began to follow the lead set by the superior officials, until at last the feeling has grown to such an extent that nothing is too bad for a Moslem paper to print about the Copts. In order to show the change of tone of which we complain, a few of the milder expressions used in the Moslem Press against the Copts are here set down:

From *Al-Alam*, March 15, 1911 :

Minorities in every country are miserable, despised by everyone, and treated like cattle. Their rights are not acknowledged nor their persons protected. Their lives are recognised as of no value, so that they sink to the lowest depths of misery.

The Coptic agitators very impolitely and

impertinently raise their voices, whereas they have
turned all Government offices into convents, where
they fill the posts with their ignorant, foolish and
diseased co-religionists, animated by that spirit of
fanaticism which has so poisoned the systems of
the high Coptic officials that it mingles with their
blood and bones. We mentioned yesterday an
example of how the theft of these posts is carried
out by the Copts.

Do not the Copts now acknowledge that by
means of their mean actions and base intrigues
they have removed the veil which hid the truth from
the eyes of the public, which truth is contained
in the fact that the Copts have been stealing the
posts from Mohammedans.

The Moslems do provide you (the Copts) with
food, and do spend money on your education.
Were it not for their money you would have remained in the lowest degree of ignorance. Why
then all this false complaint ?

From the *Egyptian Gazette*, March 17, 1911 :

Misr-el-Fatat, a popular Nationalist sheet, ad-
dresses the Copts as follows : ' Society itself will
suppress you, in spite of anything you may do,
until as a Church you are utterly decayed and
absorbed by the greater mass of the Moslem population. It is necessary to the honour both of the
nation and the Government that they should be
purely Mohammedan in character.' It continues :
' With clergymen's robes concealing their tigers'
skins and lion's claws the Copts collected their
forces to spring upon the Moslems, whose kindness

had encouraged them to this. But they failed, for
their hearts turned to water inside them. Allah,
is it possible to believe that these fools have brains
to understand with or hearts with which to feel ?
No one believes it.'

From *Al-Alam*, March 19, 1911 :

Those fanatical Copts have lately been struck
with the disease of lying ; the attack was so severe
that its cure is impossible. Their mental powers
have been so affected that they do not understand
what they say. . . . Their madness led them to
believe that their foolish demands had been ac-
cepted. They imagined that England had hoisted
its flag over Egypt, and they began to make demands dictated to them by their madness and folly.
The Egyptian Government simply laughs at their
childish actions and mad agitation. . . . It is
strange that they should dare to be so impertinent
as to make such preposterous demands.

From the *Egyptian Gazette*, March 21, 1911 :

Al-Alam, the Nationalist official organ, address-
ing the Copts, remarks : ' What is all this turmoil
and confusion, you plotting liars. It is you who
have upset yourselves by putting forward your
ridiculous claims. Where is your ambassador in
London ? Where is your Congress and your telegrams
with which you have pestered the cables all over
the world ? What has become of them all now ?
Where is the strength with which you threatened
us ? Why are you trembling with fear ? It is
time, you cowardly fanatics, to understand the

real position you occupy in this country and the
harm you have done yourselves by this evil, lying
agitation.'

From the *Egyptian Gazette*, April 4, 1911 :

A serious affray took place there (at Assiout)
on Sunday, when a Moslem wedding procession
consisting of about 200 people passed through the
Christian quarter of that city and attacked every
Copt that came in their way, inflicting severe
wounds on about twenty Copts. The Coptic Bishop
of Assiout telephoned to the Merkaz authorities, but
the latter only sent two policemen, who were only
able to arrest three of the aggressors.

From *Al-Moayad*, April 16, 1911 :

The Copts are not to be blamed, as minorities
in every country are always as far as possible
from virtue and as near as possible to vice. They
never acknowledge the many kindnesses bestowed
upon them by the majority, however clear and
apparent these are. What we suffer from them
is only a part of what we should expect on account
of their character and nature. To blame them is
to blame a madman for his madness or a passionate
man for his rage.

From the *Egyptian Gazette*, April 18, 1911 :

On the occasion of Easter, on Sunday last, a
number of low-class Moslems of Cairo organised a
procession to ridicule the Christian fêtes. The
fanatics put on some dirty black clothes to make

them appear like Coptic clergymen, and passed through the Goyara and Matbouli streets with broomsticks made in the shape of crosses and adorned with old shoes and other dirty things, shouting at the top of their voices, ' Kyrie Eleison.' The man who represented the Patriarch was a sheikh of about fifty years of age. The police arrived on the scene and made several arrests, and an official inquiry was opened afterwards at Esbekiah Caracol.

The Coptic journal *Misr* learns from Matai, Minieh, that a Moslem candidate there for the Legislative Council recently dismissed four Coptic clerks in his employment because he had gathered from high official sources that this was the best way to keep himself in favour. Our contemporary further alleges that the people of Deirout have been so stirred up by emissaries of the Moslem Congress Committee that they no longer attempt to conceal their hostility to the Copts. Statements insulting to the latter are continually being written upon the walls of the town.

From the *Egyptian Gazette*, April 27, 1911 :

A crowd of Moslems last night went to the Keneh station to see off the delegates for the Congress. After the train left the Moslems passed through the streets shouting : ' May God exalt Islam and destroy the religion of the Christians. Long live Sheikh Abdul Aziz Shawish. Down with the Coptic quarrellers.' Many of these people banged at the doors of the Christians' houses, which were, fortunately, firmly barred and bolted, as otherwise trouble would have arisen. The mob went to the

Coptic Bishop's house. The Bishop was sitting before the house with a number of well-known Copts. The Moslems mocked them and clapped their hands in derision. The Bishop at once informed the Moudir, who sent the Markaz Mamour, the Public Security officials, and a number of policemen. An inquiry was opened. This demonstration was carefully planned. It is remarkable that most of the crowd consisted of officials and omdehs (the Government superintendents of the village).

From the *African World*, May 20, 1911 :

Outrage on Copts.—An unfortunate example of fanaticism took place at Sohag on May 6. While the corpse of a Copt was being carried to burial on the back of a camel some Moslems came up and protested that it was sacrilege for the dead body of a Christian to be borne on the back of an animal which was held to be sacred and devoted to the use of the Mahmal (the litter used in the procession of the Holy Carpet). The kinsmen of the dead man tried to proceed on their way, but the Moslems hurled the dead body off the camel, breaking the coffin. The Moslems were arrested and an inquiry opened.

From *Al-Moayad*, August 3, 1911 :

Supposing that all the Christian papers supported the Copts, and that one hundred thousand Kitcheners came to Egypt, the Moslems will not be in the least affected : they will always be the occupants of the heaviest scale in Government offices and all livelihood establishments, as they are the highly educated [? Editor] majority, and the rulers of the country and masters of its real interests.

From the *Al-Moayad*, August 31, 1911 :

The Moslems will never accept even one of the Coptic demands. It is better for them to be demolished altogether than to see a Copt governing amongst them.

In connection with this extract see quotation from same paper at the beginning of this chapter.

IX

THE LIBERTY OF THE COPTIC PRESS

THE WARNING OF *AL-WATAN*

THE Copts would heartily support the authorities in putting an end to the journalistic anarchy prevailing in Egypt, but their grievance is that the Egyptian Government does not treat Moslem and Christian organs alike. This fact has been emphatically commented upon by the leading European journals in Egypt.

When the Press Law was first introduced it was felt it would be used to suppress the violence of certain journals which made it their business to stir up the feelings of their readers on political and other matters, and the Coptic Press welcomed it as a factor of peace. But once again they were mistaken, and instead of profiting in common with all peace-desiring inhabitants of Egypt by the execution of the new law they found that it placed a new weapon in the hands of their enemies.

It is my contention that it has been applied unnecessarily and with extreme harshness to the

Coptic Press. I propose to give my readers a bare outline of the circumstances under which the *Watan*, one of the two Coptic papers of Egypt, received its official warnings. The facts do not take long to recapitulate.

After the murder of Butros Pasha nearly all the persons who were subsequently arrested on the charge of making fanatical attacks upon the lives and property of Christians were pronounced insane by the Government. Two papers, one of them the principal Anglo-Egyptian journal in Egypt, the other, *Al-Watan*, published articles dealing with the subject, in which it was affirmed in identical phrases that insanity was on the increase in Egypt. No notice was taken of the article in the *Egyptian Gazette*. With *Al-Watan* it was different. The phrase was said to contain an incitement to disturbance between Copts and Moslems, and the paper received its first warning.

On the second occasion *Al-Watan* was warned for the publication of an article which dealt exclusively with Arabic literature. The attitude of the Moslem Press on this latter subject is worth repeating. The article referred to criticised the Government's decision to reprint certain medieval Arabic manuscripts. The Moslem Press arrived at the conclusion that an insult had been offered to their religion in the following manner : The book criticised was written in Arabic—so was the Koran.

Therefore the criticism must also have been directed against the Koran. Therefore the religion of Islam had been subjected to an attack by the Coptic Press. To me, and I think to many other people, this was all rather hard to understand ; but apparently the Government thought the reasoning sound, because the new law was hurried into operation, and *Al-Watan* received its second warning.

The *Egyptian Gazette*, the organ of the English community in Egypt, in commenting on the subject said :

The remarkable unanimity of the European Press in condemning this latest application of the Press Law will, it is considered, effectually prevent the Powers from consenting to hand over their subjects' privileges to the mercy of a purely Moslem censorship.

La Bourse Egyptienne, an organ of the French community in Egypt, in commenting on the same case said :

In fine, if papers are now forbidden to express their opinions freely on literary matters it would be as well to suppress the Press, and at the same time finish with the vexatious Press Law of 1881, which threatens to absorb all the time of our rulers, to the detriment of public business. For I forgot to tell you that the ' warning ' of *Al-Watan* was discussed in full Council on the 19th inst., at 3 o'clock in the afternoon, under the presidency of Mohamed Pasha Said. After all the disturbance about the Nationalist Press, as a result of the famous article in the *Dépêche Egyptienne*, one was ready to expect anything sooner than to see the Council of Ministers send a warning to a Coptic paper for having, in the twentieth century, severely criticised the Arabic literature and civilisation of the Middle Ages. Such things can only be seen in Egypt, since the end of the Pope's temporary power does not permit the Congregation of the Index to order corporal punishment or torture for authors condemned of having written subversive literature. In all truth it is time to stop ourselves on this slope of fanaticism. We, Nationalists of to-day, we, Moslem Jacobins of to-morrow, run a serious risk of being rightly accused of being upset in the rut of a Spanish or Roman inquisition.

L'Egypte, a Cairo European paper holding pronounced views in favour of the Mohammedan, wrote :

If the Government gives itself up to such abuses of power we shall have the right to demand if it wishes to re-establish slavery in Egypt.

M. Canivet, writing in the *Réforme*, says :

We do not discuss the justice and the moderation of *Al-Watan's* arguments ; we only state that its appreciations do not pass the limits permitted in Europe. Certainly the Government has been guided by an excellent thought, and we have said so, in encouraging the reprinting of old Arabic works, which constitute veritable national monuments, but we should never have thought that such books could have been considered sacred and put on the same level as the Koran. Will it not be permitted to examine them and show the amount of truth and falsehood that they contain ? How is it possible to deny that a journalist, using his right of criticism, may find such publications more harmful than useful because of the ideas that they contain, and which they might propagate in the country ? Let our ill-informed confrères, who are ready to abandon the Capitulations, judge from the example of *Al-Watan* to what perils they would be exposed. The warning to *Al-Watan* will doubtless make them reflect.

The astonishing action of the Government in condemning a paper for the publishing of an article dealing with an entirely literary subject elicited marked disapproval from even Mohammedans in Egypt. *Al-Lewa*, the well-known Islamic paper, in commenting upon it said :

Once more we protest against the Government's intervention in Press affairs while there are still law courts and judges in Egypt.

Since then the first of these manuscripts has been published, and has been found full of filthy expressions and immoral stories. *Al-Watan* drew attention to this book ('Stories of the Blind') and pointed out the truth of its former articles, for which it had been 'warned.' Finally, the Government had to withdraw the book from public sale, and the English adviser at the Ministry of Interior expressed disgust at the contents of the volume. He also confessed that *Al-Watan* had been right in its criticism and that its second warning was a mistake.

However, the said warning has not been cancelled.

X

OPINIONS OF THE BRITISH PRESS

IN this chapter I have given some extracts from articles in the leading English newspapers, which will show that the nation, as distinct from the present Government, have shown us a sympathy, for which we are grateful, and a knowledge of our position which we hope to see increased and extended among all classes of the people to whom Egypt owes so much. I have given the extracts in the order of date.

From the *Times*, September 20, 1910 :

It must be admitted that he (K. Mikhail) expresses grievances which deserve more sympathetic attention than they have yet received. The Copts represent the only Egyptian stock which can trace its descent back to the time of the Pharaohs. They form an intelligent, industrious, law-abiding community, and though their defects are undeniable, these defects are largely the result of long centuries of subjection to the often oppressive ascendancy of their Mohammedan rulers.

From the *Yorkshire Daily Observer*, September 21, 1910 :

These (Christians) in Egypt are a mere minority of the population, and it is interesting to observe that one of their spokesmen complains of the injustices which they suffer under British rule. The Moslem child, he points out, may learn his religion in the rate-aided school. But the school is doubtfully to be open to the child of the Coptic ratepayer, and still more doubtful is it whether the Koran and the Gospel will be permitted to be taught side by side.

The Copts are interesting as being the Christian descendants of the ancient Egyptians. They must have got fairly well used to oppression by this time. That is no reason why they should not have justice under British administration.

From the *Spectator*, September 24, 1910 :

The Copts are thoroughly loyal to the British rule, though according to their spokesman they have not much cause to be so. Mr. Mikhail maintains, with much appearance of truth, that the Nationalist movement is at bottom prompted by religious fanaticism. Consequently the Copts, being Christians, are the objects of constant attack at the hands of the agitators. When one of them became Prime Minister he was promptly shot by a Nationalist, and the shop of the murderer has been kept open by Nationalist money as a memorial of his heroic deed. To this danger the British officials are equally exposed, but there is a minor form of wrong which the Copts have to themselves. They do not complain, says Mr. Mikhail, that the British show them no favour because they are Christians, but they do expect to be treated on their merits, 'irrespective of any religious consideration.'

From the *Commonwealth*, October 1910 :

We hope that our readers may have seen a long letter in the *Times* of September 20th on the grievances of the Copts in Egypt. We hope to print a record of them in our November number, written by Mr. Mikhail, a Copt representative, and to urge Parliamentary inquiry into the reality of the wrongs alleged. We especially desire to know why the Copts should be refused the Government's assistance in their elementary schools, which is given to the Mohammedans. It would be pitiful if the Copts, after the gallant survival through all the long years of Moslem rule, should find the influence of England to be a more insidious enemy to their faith than the sword of Mohammed.

From the *Commonwealth*, November 1910 :

The urgency of the problem of Nationalism in Egypt must not drive us to forget the claims of our own fellow-Christians the Copts. They, if anybody, represent the ancient Egyptian people. They are indeed sons of the soil. They still reproduce the type that we can recognize on the monuments. They cannot be discarded. Mr. Kyriakos Mikhail speaks for his own people, and his article reveals the stress of their anxieties under British domination.

He asks only for equitable treatment, not for favouritism of any kind. He may well claim that the Gospel should have as good an opportunity given it in the schools as the Koran.

From the *Daily Mail*, February 17, 1911 :

Under British rule the Copts have regained some of their ancient individuality, and have begun to assert their claim to a share in the administrative work of the country. Lord Cromer recognized the justice of this claim, and did his utmost to meet it sympathetically and practically. Sir Eldon Gorst appears to have been less successful in his methods. By denying that the Copts have any cause for complaint he has succeeded in arousing them to a vigorous activity. His position, we acknowledge, is a difficult one, but for that very reason it demanded from the British administrator a wise discretion and a wise reticence. To declare, as he did on January 25th, that it ' would be the worst possible service to the Copts to treat them as a separate community ' was to invite the retort that the Copts are in fact treated by their Moslem fellow-subjects not merely as a separate but a hostile community. The antagonism between the Moslem and the Copt has been dangerously accentuated since the Nationalist movement began in Egypt. The Copts, as their telegrams show, have no wish to be treated as a separate community. But both their numbers and their religion justify the demand that their educational interests should be safeguarded. That they should contribute 32 per cent. of the taxes and yet be obliged to make special provision for the education of their children is an obvious injustice.

From the *Church Times*, February 24, 1911 :

We have received from Mr. Kyriakos Mikhail, the London representative of the Coptic Press, a most earnest appeal for sympathy with the grievances under which his race is suffering in Egypt under British administration. The Copts represent the true native stock of the Egyptians. They trace their continuous descent to the time of the Pharaohs. Through long periods of subjection and oppression they have maintained their character for intelligence and industry and respect for law. Since the time when they received the Christian faith they have preserved the Christian tradition, even if imperfectly. Even under Mohammedan rule the Copts have held high administrative rule, and if they are now complaining that they are excluded from political power it is the British authorities in Egypt that are to blame. For some inscrutable reason Lord Cromer pursued the policy of giving preference to the Moslem population, and at the present moment the Copts are the victims of injustice. Up to a comparatively recent date Christian instruction was excluded from the Government schools, and though this grievance has been remedied, yet the Christian religion may not be taught unless there is a specified number of children to receive such instruction, and their parents must pay for it as an extra. Moslems, on the contrary, are taught their religion without conditions. The teaching of the Koran is paid for by the Government, and the teaching of the Gospel by the Coptic community, which, of course, has besides to contribute to the general funds levied by the Ministry of Education. It looks as though the British Administration had adopted the Birrellian motto, ' Minorities must suffer.' We are glad to see that the protest of the Copts against this iniquitous treatment is at last attracting notice in England, and we hope that all who believe in justice will raise their voices in indignation at the discredit which the state of things we have described will deservedly bring on the English name.

From the *Daily News*, March 6, 1911 :

The grievances of the Copts obviously demand serious inquiry and consideration, and the attempt of the Egyptian Government to prevent the Copts bringing them to the notice of the Imperial Government is more intelligible than defensible.

From the *Globe*, March 7, 1911 :

It is impossible to avoid feeling a good deal of sympathy with the grievances of the Copts in Egypt. With every desire to do justice, the Government, ever since the British became masters of the country, have tended to disregard their claims to recognition, and at this moment no Copt holds a place in the Egyptian Ministry. It is true that the assassinated Premier was a Copt, but his murder, instead of bringing the position of the Copts into greater prominence, seems to have been made the excuse for neglecting them still more. The Nationalist movement in Egypt is purely Moslem, and in so

far as it has been successful both the British authorities and the Copts have suffered in credit and have
a common cause.   We need not go into details of the
Copt grievances.   It suffices to say that in the main
they relate to questions of education and the lack
of representation on the local bodies.   They are
sufficiently grave to deserve very careful attention
at the hands of the British, who have, we fancy,
somewhat hastily assumed that Egypt is as dis-
tinctly and exclusively Moslem as, say, Turkey or
Persia.   The truth is that the Copts are the representatives of the ancient Egyptian race, and have
really a better title to the country than anybody
else.   The Moslems, for all that they now greatly
outnumber the Copts in the land, are only invaders.
And the fact that the Copts comprise 40 per cent.
of the educated inhabitants of the country is one
which should prevent them from being treated as
a negligible factor in the Government.   In wealth
and education the Copts, to put it at the lowest, compare very favourably with their Moslem neighbours.

From the *Standard*, March 7, 1911 :

A serious mistake will be made by those responsible for the judicious exertion of English influence
in Egypt if the grievances of the Coptic community,
discussed by our Cairo correspondent to-day, are
ignored. . . . In spite of Sir Eldon Gorst's rather
inopportune attempt to prove that they have little
to complain of, some of the disabilities under which
the Copts labour seem indisputable.   This Christian
community, numbering about a million people, cannot be said to have shared equitably in advantages

which other races now enjoy under the reformed and more stable government which Egypt owes to foreign, and more particularly British, intervention in its affairs. . . . The old arguments which were held to justify the denial of equal rights to a people who, after all, represent the ancient population of the land will no longer hold water. The Copts have moved with the times. . . . Generally speaking, they are not allowed the chance of rising in the public service. All the Mudirs and sub-Mudirs are Mahometans. There are no Copts in the Cabinet, only two or three in the Legislative Council, and only one seat in the Provincial Councils is occupied by a Copt. They are admitted in large numbers to the lower grades of the Administration, but beyond that the racial disqualification comes into play. They may be, and often are, better educated than Mahometan candidates for promotion, but their advancement is blocked because they are Copts and Christians. It is a no less legitimate grievance that, though they contribute their fair proportion to the revenues of the State, they are debarred from educational advantages accorded to the Moslem families. Their disabilities, if stated without Oriental embellishment and without resorting to the methods of agitation which are practised by certain other Egyptian Nationalists, cannot fail to secure general and influential sympathy in this country.

From the *Evening Standard*, March 8, 1911 :

The sympathy of justice-loving Englishmen will go out to the Copts in the demands they are formulating at Assiout. Here is a section of the Egyptian population which contributes 20 per cent. of the education revenue in the provinces, yet has absolutely no say in the question of spending the money and is ruthlessly excluded from benefiting by it. The elementary schools lately established by the Government, that is by England, are Moslem schools, where the Koran is everything. Obviously there is no room here for Christians. In the Government schools in the large towns England again rides rough-shod over the feelings of these fellow-Christians of ours by prescribing Sunday examinations and Sunday attendance. These schools alone can grant the certificates that enable the boy to pass on to a professional college : the excellent Mission schools are denied the privilege. Consequently many Coptic peasants violate their consciences and send their boys to these Government schools. Even with these drawbacks this little section of the community— only 7 per cent.—provides nearly 40 per cent. of the certificate-holders.

From the *Manchester Guardian*, March 8, 1911 :

Racially the purest descendants of the ancient Egyptians, they form about 7 per cent. of the population, but their numbers are not a fair index of their energy, industry, and intelligence. It is said that they have not the same capacity for the work of administration as the Moslems, but it is admitted that so far as education and the application of it are concerned the average Copt is superior to his Moslem brother.

The Coptic grievances are then dealt with in the

order in which they were presented to the Congress, and the article concludes :

But though the problem is difficult, it is impossible not to feel that the Copts have a case which the Egyptian Government ought to meet in a serious and conciliatory spirit, and that Sir Eldon Gorst scarcely did it justice when he dismissed it so summarily a few weeks ago.

From the *Outlook* of March 11, 1911 :

While experiments are being tried it is a pity that some effort is not made to award higher appointments to the Coptic population. It is true that the Copts have had one of their standing grievances to a large extent removed by the introduction of Bible teaching into the schools (for prior to this reform the Copts had to pay for the teaching of the Koran, without any compensating advantage), but the Government still fights shy of appointing a Copt to any such position as that of Mudir. It may be admitted that the Coptic community only form a small proportion of the population, and that, having been for many years employed as clerks, they have not many among them fit for high office ; still, for all that, it would be a proper departure, and would demonstrate the impartiality of British rule for people of different religions to appoint a few Copts to some positions of administrative importance. Sir Eldon Gorst no doubt remembers the criticisms of the Moslems upon the appointment of a Copt as Prime Minister in the person of Boutros Pasha, and, weak man that he is, he now fears to do simple justice to the most loyal supporters of

British rule, in the belief that his action might cause some hostile criticisms.

In reference to the paragraph above quoted, which states that the Copts have for some years been employed as clerks, I would point out that shortly before the British occupation the Copts held many of the administrative posts under Government.

From the *Christian World*, March 16, 1911 :

It is to be hoped that instructions will be sent from London to support—and not resist—the legitimate claims of the Copts.

From the *Spectator*, April 22, 1911 :

On the matter of principle we are, however, with him [Mr. L. A. Fanous, son of Mr. Akhnoukh Fanous, a Coptic leader]. It is always the business of the British nation in countries ruled, administered or occupied by them to protect minorities and to secure their rights. Just as in India we must stand by the Mohammedan minority and see they suffer no oppression at the hands of the Hindoos, who outnumber them so greatly, so in Egypt we must stand by the Copts and Christians and safeguard them from Mohammedan oppression or neglect. Provided there are Copts competent to fill the high offices, the fact that they are not of the Mohammedan religion should not be allowed to exclude them.

From the *Morning Post*, May 2, 1911 :

British authority, wherever it extends, ought to insist upon reasonable toleration, and as between

Moslem and Christian to maintain perfect equality, choosing its administrators according to character and capacity. To adopt any other plan is to encourage in the Moslem the idea, to which he is too prone, of the impossibility of anyone but a Moslem being in any respect his equal. In its best developments Islam has been capable of toleration, and few things in the present state of the world are more disquieting than the revival in the lands of Islam of the spirit of religious fanaticism. This is a matter in regard to which the British Government and the British nation have a responsibility, which they may try to evade, but from which they cannot escape.

From the *Standard*, May 2, 1911 :

There may still be a doubt in some quarters as to the genuineness of Coptic grievances, but the facts have only to be known to be appreciated, and they cannot be always concealed. The Copts, who after all stand for the ancient population of Egypt, are asking for no more than what is their due. . . . The hardships under which the Copts suffer are not rendered more endurable by a recollection of the fact that in some respects they were better off in days when no Christian Power interfered in Egyptian affairs. When Mohamed Ali Pasha ruled the land the finances were in the hands of a Copt. Copts likewise filled high administrative posts in the provinces. During the reign of Ismail Pasha the War Office was controlled by a Copt : a member of the same community was head of the Khedivial household. The Mudir of one of the provinces was a Copt. Within recent years a Copt, in the person of the murdered Boutros Pasha, has been Prime

Minister : and the advancement of this capable and
patriotic Egyptian would by itself be a sufficient
reply to the arguments that Copts lack the qualities
which must be regarded as indispensable for the
proper discharge of important duties. As a matter
of fact, the Copt is not inferior to the Egyptian
Moslem in intelligence, in education, or in administrative ability. He does not ask for exceptional
treatment, but only for equality.

Again, on May 11, 1911, in criticising the British
Agent's report, the *Standard's* leading article contains a concise refutation of this attempt to pass
over our claims as being non-existent :

It is not easy to follow the Agent's account of
the relations between Copts and Mohammedans.
Referring to the alarm created among the Copts
by the assassination of Boutros Pasha, he remarks
that this community is always ready to cry out
before it is hurt. There was never, he declares,
any real cause for uneasiness ; yet in almost the
same breath he considers it a matter of surprise that
no serious collision occurred in view of the attempts
made to incite the people to violence. As for the
very reasonable demands which the Copts have
advanced for fairer treatment, Sir Eldon Gorst
takes up a partisan attitude which we cannot help
thinking is altogether incompatible with the obligations of strict impartiality incumbent on the representative of British authority in Egypt. To the
complaint that the Christian Copt is denied admission to the higher grades in the public service he
replies by quoting statistics showing the use that is

made of them in the lower grades, and by laying it
down as a general axiom that the Copt, though an
admirable clerk, financier, and man of business,
lacks a natural aptitude for high executive work.
Yet in a previous paragraph he had referred to
Boutros Pasha's Premiership as refuting the allegation that capable Copts are debarred from holding
high office. Again, he says that as time goes on
it may become feasible to satisfy this particular
demand, and he entirely agrees that no other
criterion than merit should exist. The Copts contend that if promotion is to go by merit the time
has already arrived for relieving them of a disability
based, not, as Sir E. Gorst says, on any natural
inaptitude, but on their religion. On one point,
it may be added, he is either misinformed or has
chosen to use words which cannot fail to create a
wrong impression. The Congress at Assiout numbered, we are asked to believe, ' 500 members or
more.' Photographs of the Assembly show that
over 1200 must have attended. The movement,
indeed, is so far from being insignificant that it
would be necessary to deal at greater length with
this part of the Agent's report had not the question
of Copt grievances been already discussed in connection both with their own Congress and the
Mahometan meeting at which Riaz Pasha presided
the other day.

From the *Yorkshire Daily Observer*, May 15,
1911 :

If it is true, as alleged, that the high positions are closed to the Copts simply because of

their religion, the grievance is one that seems to us incapable of defence, and we fail to see what objection can be made to the plea that Coptic officials should be enabled to observe the Christian Sabbath by regulations that would allow them to render compensatory service on other days of the week.

From the *Birmingham Post*, of May 13th, 1911, the following extracts are taken :

The Copts, who are the descendants of the ancient inhabitants of the country, though a minority, form no inconsiderable section of the population. They have petitioned the authorities for more considerate and fairer treatment as a community than has hitherto been extended to them.   But their representations have met with scant official encouragement, while the recital of their communal disabilities has been considered by a body of Moslems only to be rejected as unfounded or impossible of redress in the racial and religious conditions of the country. . . . We are glad to be able to say that up to the present the Copts have shown that they are gifted with an admirable perception of what may properly be done to attract attention to their particular complaints. . . . The British Agent has not been greatly impressed by the gravity of the grievances of the Copts, and appears to have been somewhat misled concerning them during the course of certain personal enquiries he thought it necessary to make. . . . Nevertheless, though from the standpoint of the British Agent the Coptic leaders might not be congratulated on the first-fruits of their agitation, they achieved something in securing a clear exposition of their case. The more one considers the statement of their disabilities the more one finds it difficult to understand how Sir Eldon Gorst could be persuaded that these Egyptian Christians ' have no real grievances of any importance.' Their own representations show that, in the first place, they have a grievance which concerns the practice of their religion. Moreover, they suffer under a serious educational disability in being taxed for the maintainance of institutions which their children may not attend. But apart from inequality of treatment which may be attributed to considerations purely religious, they are, as a minority, seriously handicapped in regard to the positions to which they may aspire in the administration of their country. . . . Members of the community occupy numerous minor official appointments, but they are rigorously debarred from admission to higher berths which they may be qualified to fill. . . . Yet it is a fact beyond dispute that in the days before any Western European Power was closely involved in Egyptian affairs, Copts held high executive appointments. Much more recent was the case of the murdered Prime Minister, Boutros Pasha—a Copt—whose assassination was undeniably the outcome of Nationalist propaganda.

From the *Daily Chronicle*, May 16, 1911 :

The Government's unreasonable attitude of hostility to the Copts, who have always been firm supporters of its authority and order in Egypt, and its shameless truckling to the worst and most despicable manifestations of Chauvinistic fanaticism and reactionary ideas at the dictation of the Moslem Press, which is notorious for its hostility to established authority in Egypt, are only one cause of the many which have been active in the production of the present critical situation in the country, the keynote of which is uncompromising hostility to modern progressive ideas of true Liberalism and nationality.

From the *Belfast Evening Telegraph*, July 14, 1911:

Obviously, then, the former [the Copts] are able to make out a strong case for themselves, and while in all ages and nations religious difficulties have been the hardest to compose, still it is scarcely worthy of our Government, which admittedly has done so much for the betterment of the Egyptians, to leave these matters unsettled and be a source of friction and animosity between the two great sections of the population of the country. While holding the scale between all sections and parties as evenly as possible, according to our national traditions, if we take any side it ought to be that of the weak against the strong ; but in this case we seem to have reversed this order and appear to be favouring the strong against the weak. This is not creditable to our present Government.

From the *Evening Times*, September 23, 1911 :

Amongst the problems that await Lord Kitchener's attention in Egypt, the Coptic question is not among the least. The Copts complain that Moslems are favoured at their expense in such subjects as taxation, representation, and appointments to high official positions. In March last a deputation of leading Copts attempted to lay these grievances before the Khedive, but that Prince refused to receive them, a rebuff for which they blamed the late Sir Eldon Gorst, who, in his annual report, subsequently published some stinging, and we think prejudiced, comments on the Coptic cause.

The Copts are the Egyptian Christians, the oldest body of the faith of the Cross in the world, and the descendants of the inhabitants of the country in the days of the Pharaohs. The average Mahometan, on the other hand, if we except Turkish colonists, has for ancestors the Arabs who conquered Egypt in the eighth century. There is often little in appearance to distinguish a Copt from a Moslem ; for the most part, however, the Copts are much fairer than Moslems of Arab blood. The men of both parties dress alike, except the priests, when the Copts' robes of sombre hue and plain stuff contrast with the gorgeous coloured silken ' Kaftan ' worn by Arab sheikhs. Coptic women, with few exceptions, wear the black ' habara,' or hooded mantle, like their Moslem sisters, but, unlike them, go with unveiled faces.

The Copts are a brainy people, as befits the progeny of the architects who planned the Pyramids and the buildings of lovely Philæ, and of the king in remote days who knew how to float a stone temple down the Nile waterway. Mercilessly persecuted by the conquerors of the dark ages, they have survived to keep their footing to-day.

Copts, not Arabs, built, by order of Caliphs, those mosques which are the wonder and delight of the select company of archæologists and of thousands of Cook's tourists. Behind massive walls in the dusty streets of old Cairo stand the Coptic churches, most ancient in the world, rich with ivory and ebony, and the home of stately and curious ritual.

Living quietly, and submitting as much as possible to the customs of the Mahometan conquerors, the Copts have been lawyers, architects, clerks, goldsmiths, and money-lenders for generations. They have generally dwelt in their own quarters of the towns. These, in up-country districts, are still walled, though the custom of closing the gates at sunset has passed away. There are no inter-marriages between Copts and Mahometans, but business friendships are not uncommon. The Egyptian Christians have often been the object of Moslem jealousy, and in the days of a certain Caliph a decree was issued forbidding their employ-ment in Government offices. This law, however, was quickly repealed, as it was soon seen that the business side of things did not work smoothly without their industry, energy, and punctual habits. To-day, when the native tramwaymen or postmen go off duty the Moslem will probably spend his leisure at a café, playing draughts or talking politics. A Copt in the same employment is likely to be taking a lesson in French or English, paid for out of his scanty earnings.

Ismail Pacha quite understood the useful

qualities of his Coptic subjects, and extended them his favour. A Moslem minister once spoke, grumblingly, in the Pacha's presence, of a certain mudir as ' this Coptic official,' but was told abruptly that ' all were Egyptian alike.'

In Lord Cromer's day the successes of Copts at Government examinations gave the British Agent reason to reproach Moslems, in order to stimulate them, and compare them unfavourably with their Christian colleagues. Piqued vanity encouraged the ill-feeling that never lay long dormant. Little by little it has become stronger, until the Copts have now considerable reason for complaint. And although in past days they were often admitted to high posts, they have not had their due in this matter of late. There are, and have been, exceptions—the late Butros Pacha among the number —but it often happens that Copts are put aside for their religion alone.

Copts are never, nowadays, given the posts of governor or mudir (a kind of lesser governor). The objection that a Copt could not rule over Mahometan fellahin does not hold good. The fellah is a quiet-living creature, who only asks to be allowed to gain his living peaceably. Whether his over-lord be Coptic landowner or Mahometan mudir is all one to him.

Though I do not propose to make use of many extracts from the letters which have appeared from time to time from individuals in the English Press, the following, written by such an eminent authority as Dr. A. J. Butler, which appeared in the *Times* of February 20, 1911, will, I think, be of interest to my readers as throwing a light upon the question of Coptic grievances. The telegram referred to in this letter is that quoted in another chapter from the columns of the *Times* :

SIR,—The very temperate and influential telegram which you publish from the Copts in Upper Egypt should help people in this country to appreciate the truth concerning the educational and other grievances of the Copts. The issue has been ignored or obscured in almost every communication from Egypt which of late has appeared in the London Press. It is this—that at present the Copts are the victims of a differential treatment, that they demand only equality of treatment, and that the demand is steadily refused by the Government of Egypt. The Copts ask for even justice and equal opportunity with their Moslem fellow-citizens. The refusal of this elementary right is injurious to the peace and well-being of Egypt, and it is against all the principles of liberty on which British government is founded.—I am, Sir, yours faithfully,

                                          A. J. BUTLER.
BRASENOSE COLLEGE, OXFORD.

In the October (1910) number of the *Nineteenth Century* Dr. A. J. Butler had previously contributed an article on Egyptian affairs, from which the following extracts are taken :

The first great error of British policy has been to give preferential instead of impartial treatment to the Mohammedan part of the population. It is this which has had the effect of kindling fanaticism. The error began, it is fair to say, with Lord Cromer. He was in most ways the ideal ruler for Egypt—capable, strong, fearless, high-minded, and, above all, just. But no man is infallible, and the mistake of unduly favouring the Moslems—a mistake which he would have discovered and corrected if he had remained in power—was adopted by his successor and followed to the edge of disaster. There can only be one true policy in dealing with the people of Egypt—to hold the scales in even balance and to ensure equal rights and equal opportunities for the various classes and creeds of the community. . . . The favouritism displayed towards the Moslems may be illustrated in various ways. At the time of the British Occupation many, if not most, of the subordinate offices in the Government services were held by Copts. Since that date the number of Christian Civil Servants has steadily diminished, the vacant places being filled by Moslems, while higher offices in the Interior, such as Moudir and Mamour, are entirely closed to Christians.

A letter, signed ' A. B. Sayce,' which appeared in the *Saturday Review*, August 6, 1910, contains the appended reference to the Coptic claim for administrative posts :

In favour of the claim of the Copts to government leadership in the future, it ought to be borne in mind that all through the centuries of Mohammedan persecution they contrived to keep the actual administration of the country in their own hands. It was not until the English Occupation that they were deprived of the higher posts. At the present moment the Inspector-General of the Postal Administration is a Copt, and it is admitted by some, who are by no means inimical to the existing regime, that this is one of the few well-managed administrations in Egypt.

Mr. Edward Fothergill, who was formerly acting editor of the *Egyptian Gazette*, in a letter to the *Pall Mall Gazette*, on March 17, 1911, writes:

The Copt, on the other hand, has been losing slowly but surely his hold upon public affairs. Year by year he sees posts formerly occupied by Copts getting vacant, only to see them filled by Moslems. For all his wealth and for all his patriotism he is really thrust into the position of an outsider, with no more voice in public matters than that of a Greek grocer. . . . He asks, and surely with some reason, for that share in the administration of his country for which his wealth and his talents fit him.

The following are extracts from an article, which appeared in the *Nineteenth Century* of September 1911, by Dr. A. J. Butler:

At the Arab conquest of Egypt, as already stated, the Copts passed under the rule of Islam by a treaty which guaranteed them in the possession of their religion and their churches, and promised them protection. They became what is technically known as *Ahl adh Dhimmah*, or People of Protection. They were known also to their Arab conquerors under another name—*Ahl al Kitab*, or People of the Book— i.e. people whose religion is founded on Holy Writ as opposed to Pagans.

The story of the relations between Christians and Muslims during the period of 1270 years which has elapsed since the conquest is naturally a somewhat chequered one. From the beginning very great moral and social, and very great financial, pressure was put upon all Christians to change their religion, since by turning Muslims they became equals and brothers of the conquerors, instead of being subjects, and they escaped payment of the poll-tax. Moreover, the Christians were at all times liable to suffer from cruel extortion and persecution at the hands of irresponsible Arab rulers, under whose orders every kind of violent outrage and ignominy were heaped upon the Christians, who were robbed and murdered, while their churches were plundered and destroyed. That some of the Christians went over to Mohammedanism, in fear of their lives, is far less wonderful than the fact that so large a part, by their stubborn endurance, were able to withstand the fires of persecution and to carry their faith through the flames scatheless.

But the two peoples could not have existed side by side so long in the same country unless there had been a considerable amount of friendly feeling between them. And there is plenty of evidence of this feeling in the Arabic and Coptic chronicles ; evidence so striking that I may be pardoned for illustrating it by examples chosen from successive periods of history.

In the seventh century not only were the Christians not 'reduced to slavery' by the conquest, but the command of the Prophet Mohammed was so well remembered by the Muslims that they promoted Christians to the very highest offices of State in Egypt. Thus in A.D. 670 the Governorship of Alexandria was held by a Christian, Theodore, who, strangely enough, was a Melkite, and therefore unfriendly to the Copts. Ten years later Theodore's son was Governor, but either an adherent of the Coptic faith or under Coptic influence. At the same time it was Coptic secretaries who administered the affairs of Alexandria : the Commissioner (Metawali) of Alexandria was a Copt : so was Theophanes, the Governor of Mariut, or Mareotis ; and we read that Abd al Aziz, the Muslim Governor-General or Viceroy, appointed two Coptic Secretaries of State 'over the whole land of Egypt, and Mariut, and Marakiah, and Pentapolis '—i.e. all Western Egypt and the region of Barca and Cyrene. A little later, about A.D. 705, Athanasius, a Copt, was President of the Diwan at Misr (or Cairo), and responsible for the collection of taxes—head of the Department of Inland Revenue : all the secretaries in the Department were Copts, and a Copt, called Butrus, held the exalted position of Governor of Upper Egypt.

.   .   .   .   .

So the story runs on, the Copts being treated alternately with favour and ferocity, yielding here and there, even in masses, to the pressure of persecution, yet on the whole upholding their faith with a grandeur of courage which few peoples have rivalled. And all through there is seen a background of friendly relations with Muslims and Muslim rulers.

Thus the Caliph Khamarawaih delighted to visit the monastery of Kusair, near Cairo, where he stood often in rapt admiration of the splendid gold and coloured mosaics in the Church of the Apostles; and he built there an upper room, with windows on all four sides for enjoyment of the view over city and mountains and desert.

．　　　．　　　．　　　．　　　．　　　．

The same good relations prevail to-day in country places. The rebuilding of Coptic churches by the early Caliphs has its analogy in our own day in the building of mosques by wealthy Copts for their Muslim neighbours on some of the large estates in Upper Egypt.

．　　　．　　　．　　　．　　　．　　　．

But there is a further lesson from history, a lesson which has been strangely overlooked, but one which should come home to the Muslims with all the force of irresistible authority. For their prophet Mohammed himself upon his deathbed laid on his followers the solemn injunction to regard the Copts as kinsmen, and to give them kind and friendly treatment. This remarkable incident is among the best attested of the Muslim traditions, and the evidence for it is derived from Muslim sources. The ninth-century history of the conquest of Egypt by Ibn Abd al Hakam—a work still unpublished from the Paris MS.—gives the substance of an address delivered by Amr Ibn al Asi, the conqueror of Egypt, upon Friday in Easter week of 644. In the course of it Amr said :

'Take good care of your neighbours, the Copts, for Omar, the Commander of the Faithful, told me that he heard the Apostle of God say : " God will open Egypt to you after my death." So take good care of the Copts in that country ; for they are your kinsmen and under your protection. Cast down your eyes, therefore, and keep your hands off them.'

Ashhab Ibn Abd al Aziz is quoted as giving the command of Mohammed thus : ' Take charge of the Copts of Egypt, for you will find among them useful auxiliaries against your enemy.' Umm Salimah reported the Prophet's words in the same language : 'God ! God commits the Copts of Egypt to your charge ; for you shall rule over them, and they shall be to you an increase of numbers and a body of helpers in the path of God.' When asked how the Copts should help the Muslims in religion, Mohammed answered : ' They shall relieve you of the affairs of this world, and so leave you free for religious worship,' *i.e.* they will conduct the actual administration of the Government, superintending the taxation and collection of revenue in particular. Mohammed also said : ' Take care of the men with the curling hair, the Copts of Egypt, for they are your uncles and kinsmen ' : and Abdullah, the son of Amr, used to quote Mohammed as having said : ' The Copts are the noblest of foreigners, the gentlest of them in behaviour, the most excellent in character, the nearest in kinship to the Arabs and to the tribe of the Kuraish in particular.' Traditions of this kind, in which the Copts are called a 'protected people' occur in Tabari, Al Kindi, As Suyuti, Abu 'l Mahasin, and other Arab historians, and may be regarded as thoroughly well-established.

.   .   .   .   .   .

After commenting on the 'warning' of *Al-Watan* Dr. Butler goes on :

The truth is that the Government refuse to admit the claim of the Copts to equality of treatment, which is all they claim. They are an integral portion of the population, though a minority— Egyptians among the Egyptians — and entitled to be so regarded. Before the law and before the Government there should be in strict justice neither Copts nor Muslims, but one community of Egyptians.

.   .   .   .   .   .

The story of the Coptic Congress is then told, and the writer comments :

The whole atmosphere of the Congress was friendly to the Muslims, and the discussion of the Coptic disabilities was extremely temperate. Nor was there the slightest sign of local hostility or disturbance. So far, however, from appreciating the moderation of the Coptic demands or reciprocating the desire for friendly relations, the organs of the Nationalist Press have made the Congress an excuse for a display of violent intolerance and abuse of the Copts. One of the worst offenders is the

Alexandrian *Al-Ahali*, which is known to be the
organ of the Minister of the Interior. This paper
had long before the Congress distinguished itself by
the bitter intemperance of its language against the
Copts ; but then it belonged to or was sheltered by
a Nationalist Minister, and so was privileged to lead
a campaign of violence, which can have no object
but to destroy the peace of the community. Against
all this the thunders of the Press law are silent ; *Al-
Ahali* may preach strife and violence and disruption
of the State, while *Al-Watan* is threatened with
extinction for a mild essay in literary criticism.

One is driven back time after time to the same
point and the same conclusion—that there is no
equality of treatment and no desire to give equality
of treatment, on the part of the Government, which
is administered in sympathy with overt Nationalism.
This is not the place to catalogue the grievances of
the Copts, but one of them is the educational
grievance, which was set out in a former article in
this ' Review ' (October 1910). I may add that
Coptic teachers are not sent to Europe to complete
their training, as Muslim teachers are. During the
last twenty years only four Copts—two in 1907 and
two in 1908—have been sent to England among
all the students of the Egyptian Educational
Mission in England. No Coptic teacher has been
promoted head-master, or vice-principal, or sub-
inspector, to any of the Government schools, and no
Copt has been given the post of director or sub-
director to any of the various offices in the Ministry
of Education, although some of the Coptic clerks
in the Ministry hold teaching diplomas ; whereas
many of the Muslims who are promoted over their

head to more lucrative and responsible posts have no certificates at all. The disparity of treatment is really very great : and the most inveterate enemy of the Copts cannot say that in point of education or of intellectual capacity they are inferior to the Muslims. So, too, in the other branches of the Government service. It is sheer injustice to close the higher posts in the service to Copts, instead of providing an open career to talent or merit regardless of religion.

In Sir Eldon Gorst's last Report an attempt is made to refute the allegation of unfair treatment by giving statistics of the number of Copts in Government service. It is there calculated that the number of Copts employed is greater in proportion than the number of Muslims. But these statistics—whoever compiled them—are not free from bias. Thus the tables include all Copts who hold non-pensionable offices and exclude all Muslims who hold the like. Moreover, the Copts from ancient days have inherited a capacity for office work which the Muslims do not possess in the same measure ; and the Copts often accept laborious and ill-paid posts which Muslims disdain. But, even if the statistics were true, they are beside the mark, for the grievance remains that the avenue of promotion to the highest offices is closed to the Copts, and that for the Copts ability and merit in these days are no passport to reward.

Sir Eldon Gorst last January proclaimed his opinion that it would be rendering a very ill service to the Copts to treat them as a separate community. That is very true ; but its truth is a verdict in condemnation of the Government. For it is the

Government, and the Government alone, who make the distinction. The whole burden of the Coptic case is that the Government does treat them as a separate community, and does discriminate against them. The Coptic Congress has been followed by an Islamic Congress in Cairo ; but its purpose was only to protest against the Coptic claim to justice and to assert the privileges possessed by the Muslim population.

XI

THE APPOINTMENT OF LORD KITCHENER

On July 15, 1911, the Press announced the official appointment of Lord Kitchener as British Agent and Consul-General in Egypt. Most of the British newspapers have expressed their opinion in favour of the appointment, and have declared that the fact of Lord Kitchener going to Egypt will impress the so-called Nationalists—those whose propaganda is that the British must leave Egypt at once. I was of this opinion before I read some most interesting articles in the Egyptian Press. According to these the two influential parties in Egypt—namely, the Nationalist Party and the Party of the People— are rather pleased at the prospect of an Agent-General who, as they anticipate, will not be on such friendly terms with the Khedive as was Sir Eldon Gorst. Friendship between the Khedive and the British Agent they regard as being bad for their cause, and for this reason they are not sorry about the new appointment.

The opinion of *Al-Moayad* on this point is apparently not yet quite settled. This paper

obtains its influence, not from the number of people
it circulates amongst, but from being known as
the organ of the Palace. The same thing might be
said of *Al-Ahali*, which owes its existence to the
supposition that it is the organ of the Premier.
But the influence of these two papers is limited,
and they are only read for the semi-official views
they express. The Moslems of Egypt consider both
papers as being traitors to their country ; and in
proof of this they point to the fact that both are
under the thumbs of those who are themselves
under the thumb of the British Agent.

To recognise that Egyptians are rather satisfied with the appointment of Lord Kitchener, one
has only to allude to the views of the Nationalist
Party, which forms about 80 per cent. of the
Moslems of Egypt, and those of the Copts, the
native Christians, who are a most important section
of the population.

In a speech to a large audience at Cairo, on
September 14, 1911, Mohammed Bey Farid, the
famous leader of the Nationalist party, declared
that

the appointment of Lord Kitchener has only
frightened those who seek for personal advantages
and private interests, even though the result might
be the ruin of their country : those running after
office, only for the sake of notoriety or money ;
those who seek influence that they may use it

against their political enemies, however friendly they may have been with them before getting into office.

Abd-el-Hamid Bey Ammar, another great supporter of the Nationalist party, says in *Al-Alam*, September 11 :

Our governors who have just enjoyed influence and independence in their methods, did not rightly use the weapon placed in their hands. Instead of taking advantage of the circumstances to do good to their nation and justice to their people, and thus prove to the country what would be the rule of her sons, they practised during their rule different kinds of harshness. The chiefs allowed those under them to do as they liked, and paid no attention to their greediness, their unfairness, or their insults, showing the people that they had confidence in these men and were satisfied with them and their actions.

Even the most fanatical papers seem to recognise the corruption and injustice that has prevailed in the country, and they warmly welcome the appointment of Lord Kitchener on account of his reputation for justice and impartiality.

In reply to questions on the appointment, in the House of Commons, on July 18, 1911, Sir Edward Grey stated :

I am confident that the qualities possessed by Lord Kitchener, his special knowledge and experience of Egyptian affairs, and his impartiality and capacity, make the appointment one that should command general confidence. . . . The appointment to Egypt is an extremely difficult one to fill, as everybody knows, and requires special knowledge, special experience, and special qualities. I do not know anyone who possesses these special qualities, special knowledge, and special experience in so high a degree as Lord Kitchener. . . . Of course, before Lord Kitchener goes to Egypt the policy to be followed in Egypt, and the questions that have to be dealt with in Egypt, will be the subject of discussion between him and His Majesty's Government.

The Coptic organs have on several occasions shown their satisfaction at the appointment, and declared that though they did not know whether Lord Kitchener was going to redress the Coptic grievances or not, the statement of Sir Edward Grey was very satisfactory to them, as they lay great stress on his allusion to the new Agent's ' impartiality.'

We hope also that the harsh and exceptional laws that have been put in practice during the last few years will be cancelled. I allude to the Deportation Law, which gives power to a Court of Assize to deport an accused person against whom it has not found evidence for conviction, and the Press Law, by which the Government may suppress a newspaper without hearing any defence or explanation. The presence of these laws seems to me to be a sign of weakness rather than of firmness. This is proved by the fact that in the time of Lord Cromer the country was peaceful and orderly without the operation of such laws. The increase of crime, which led to the introduction of these laws, was due to negligence on the part of those who are responsible for watching the working and administration of the laws of the country ; and had it been met with firmness at the beginning there would have been no need for the stringent measures adopted after it had got out of hand. Putting such laws into practice at the moment when the Egyptian was supposed to be progressing towards self-govern-ment is a peculiar method of marking his progress. To me it seems to denote retrogression, not progress.

Those who desire to defend the policy pursued in Egypt during the last few years have a very difficult duty to perform. This is felt by everyone, both in Egypt and England, with the exception of those very few persons who have profited by the policy, i.e. the native Egyptian high authorities, who have been granted a free hand, after being entirely tied down under Lord Cromer ; and those who are used by them as their instruments in Eng-land. I can find no better word than ' anarchy ' to describe the state of affairs that has lately prevailed in Egypt. Appointments have been given to those who are neither capable nor deserv-ing. Liberty has disappeared, and in its place has arisen a system of persecution and intrigue, which has become one of the principal means employed in governing the country. The weak are oppressed by the strong and influential, and those in office have taken advantage of their position to further their own ends. The Copts and Moslems, friendly enough some few years ago, are now at enmity with each other. Members of the Provincial Councils are interested in certain newspapers, which they support by the use of public money paid for alleged official advertisements in their columns. Already a petition has been sent to Lord Kitchener by a wealthy Moslem of Akhmim, Ghirgeh Province, giving the facts of a special case in which he was the victim, and pointing out that unfortunate landowners in Egypt are forced to pay out exorbitant sums to certain societies and newspapers favoured by the Government authorities. Very few dare refuse to submit to this kind of blackmail, and landowners who desire to escape persecution are therefore compelled to pay up and keep quiet about it. Within the last few days another instance of bribery and persecution has been reported by *Journal Misr*, which even eclipses the instance given in the petition to Lord Kitchener. Owing to the epidemic of the cotton worm it has become necessary for the Government to take steps to find a way of getting rid of the plague, and to use some method of compulsion in order to make people work in the fields, and to get them to work in those parts of the country where the presence of the pest is in greatest need of attention. The power of compulsion has therefore been placed in the hands of the Omdehs (village authorities), and they have proceeded to use it according to their lights. In one instance, on July 30, 1911, at Ed-Douer, Assiout Province, the Omdeh collected a few Sheikhs (Omdeh's assistants) and some helpers and went round the place capturing by force every male they could lay their hands on. When a large number of men had been got together by this impromptu pressgang the Omdeh proceeded to survey the crowd and find reasons, chiefly financial, why some should be taken and others left. The payment of £E.25, with other considerations in the way of cereals, cheese, and other foodstuffs, was sufficient to obtain the release of some three-quarters of the prisoners. Of the others, it appeared that out of fifty captured some ten were Moslems and the rest Copts, which seems to be rather a large proportion in a place where the Moslems are very greatly in excess of the Copts in numbers. Also, another peculiarity was that most of the men seized happened to be not field-hands or labourers, but merchants and artisans ; that is to say, not those who would be most likely to be of use in working in the fields, but those who might possibly be most inclined to pay in order to get out of the task. However, as they did not succeed in satisfying the Omdeh, many of them have had to go on to the fields and leave their families destitute. Many instances of this sort are reported to the same paper from Copts in other villages. The correspondents state that the Copts there imagined that they had gone back to the dark days of the persecution.

If further proof is needed of the failure of the recent policy, there is more to be found for the looking. During the last few years the influence of the political agitator has greatly increased; the murder of the Premier was one of its results. In business matters also the weakness of the administration and the insecurity felt alike by natives and Europeans was shown in the financial crisis that took place and by the fact that the price of land has fallen greatly. But perhaps the most striking proof of the state of anarchy prevailing is that at the present time there is proceeding in the Egyptian papers a hot debate on the subject of the impartiality of the judges, and it is openly alleged that the Egyptian judges are biased in favour of their co-religionists. A nation is indeed in a bad way when even the scales of Justice are suspected of being out of balance.

Sir Edward Grey has taken upon the shoulders of the Government the responsibility for this state of things by his statement that the attacks made upon the late Agent-General ' ought never to have been made upon him. They ought to have been made upon the Government, on whose instructions he acted, if they were to be made at all.' I am very glad to understand that he now proposes to end it and seek for a proper means of helping the Egyptians on towards self-government.

Lord Cromer had no confidence in the native officials and did not rely upon them in the least. Therefore during his time the Egyptian official, generally speaking, was simply an instrument in the hands of the British official. He was not given the chance to use his intelligence.

Mr. J. M. Robertson stated in the House of Commons, on July 27, 1911, that the recent policy had been criticised because its tendency was to appoint competent native Egyptians to Government positions instead of giving every appointment to Englishmen. As a matter of fact, the number of British officials was not reduced nor were native Egyptians appointed according to capability. Facts recorded in other chapters of this book are sufficient to prove this. The only change that took place was that when Lord Cromer's successor arrived he found the Egyptians crying out that they were shut out from all influence in the governing of their country, and to satisfy them he gave great power to the Egyptian high officials, who, badly chosen and unused to the exercise of such authority, naturally misused the influence so injudiciously given them.

We hope that Lord Kitchener will appoint native Egyptians to a large number of the minor posts under Government now filled by Europeans. There are numbers of natives quite capable of filling these positions, and as they gained experience in Government work and methods they could be moved up to higher posts. It is difficult to understand in what other way the native Egyptian is ever to gain the necessary experience to enable him to govern his country unless he is allowed to start at the bottom and work up to the more responsible positions as he shows himself capable of filling them, and it is still more difficult to understand why there are such great numbers of minor offices occupied by foreigners and entirely closed to natives of the country quite as competent. There is also a method at present in vogue in the Egyptian Government to keep certain posts exclusively for British officials, and this line of demarcation often prevents an Egyptian occupying a Government position for which he is fitted.

But it is a well-known fact in Egypt that Lord Kitchener, when in charge of the Egyptian army, treated all his officers alike, whatever their creed or nationality. This is a striking proof of his impartiality, and it is this admitted characteristic that gives us reason to hope that the class distinctions and bad feeling between British and native, Copt and Moslem, which have increased and flourished so considerably, will under his control finally disappear.

We may have hopes that not only will the present wrongs be righted, but that steps will be taken to institute a real spirit of progress. It is very apparent that no nation can ever progress or prosper while its whole energies are spent in political agitation. The time for that is past, and the Egyptians must turn their attention to the serious side of providing means by which the population may earn its livelihood. At present the chief product of the country is cotton; but no nation can live entirely on the production of one article of commerce. Ample evidence exists that a Department of Commerce and Industries is badly needed. There is great scope for inventions to be worked out and practical industries and manufactures founded, but no encouragement is given, nor is any means provided, for the creation or use of inventive skill, and the consequence is a feeling that the British exploit the country for themselves and check local manufactures.

Sanitation, especially in the towns, is a subject of very great importance. The present state of affairs is shown by the high death rate and the great mortality among children that prevails. At present nothing seems to be done to cope with this evil effectually.

There is a great want of technical and trade

schools where Egyptian boys may be taught to earn their living in some practical profession. The effect of the present system of education is that the only future in front of the children is the hope that they may be able to secure some minor and ill-paid post in the Civil Service. The institution of a Department of Commerce would do much to change all this, and the creation of such a Department should be one of the first points in any policy that has for its object the well-being and progress of the Egyptian nation.

THE END